How our faith interacts with our digital world is such an important topic, and this book gives us the theological foundations we need, whilst also being intensely practical. I wish all Christians would read this!
Andy Geers, PrayerMate app developer

Our generation is faced with both the privilege and the responsibility to make the most of this unique moment in time. As we leverage technology to share the gospel in new ways, we encounter the inevitable questions that come with any uncharted territory. In *Virtually Human*, Pete Nicholas and Ed Brooks do a great job of fully examining the complexity of this landscape, and invite us to grapple with the important issues that arise at the intersection of faith, technology and humanity.
Bobby Grunewald, Creator of YouVersion & Innovation Leader at LifeChurch.tv

Technology advances at a pace far faster than even leading technology authorities can comprehend, and the moral and societal implications of these developing technologies feel more like science fiction than science. The church is in desperate need of intelligent voices to help navigate through the complexities connected with digital technology. This book exposes the fallacy of the neutrality of technology and carefully navigates between the extremes of the pro- and anti-technology voices. Grounded in a rich biblical theology, Peter Nicholas and Ed Brooks have served the church in presenting a gospel-grounded framework from which we can begin to approach the wonder and terror of technology.
David Kim, Executive Director, Center for Faith & Work, Redeemer Presbyterian Church, New York

Virtually Human masterfully steers clear of the typical pitfalls of writing on a subject like this. It is measured without once being boring; prophetic without being scolding; and accessible without being simplistic. Ed and Pete are equally expert in their command of theology and technology. I especially appreciated their exploration of the currencies of technology – time, community, identity, knowledge and so on – by reframing them around the biblical narrative. Their arguments and illustrations are so strong and self-evident that I can imagine this book being equally effective for the Christian or the sceptic.
Scott Kauffman, Vice President of Content and Strategy at Redeemer Presbyterian New York

Our digital world can leave us bewitched, bothered and bewildered. Simplistic answers don't satisfy. The strength of Ed and Pete's analysis is its theological muscle, which has the power to slow down our spinning compass and to redirect us clearly and gloriously towards Jesus Christ. Read it and get ready for real, not virtual, transformation.

Daniel Strange, Academic Vice Principal, Oak Hill College, London

VIRTUALLY
HUMAN

VIRTUALLY
HUMAN

Flourishing in a digital world

ED BROOKS &
PETE NICHOLAS

INTER-VARSITY PRESS
Norton Street, Nottingham NG7 3HR, England
Email: ivp@ivpbooks.com
Website: www.ivpbooks.com

First published 2015

British Library Cataloguing in Publication Data
A catalogue record for this book is available from the British Library.

ISBN: 978-1-78359-389-7

Set in Dante 12/15 pt
Typeset in Great Britain by CRB Associates, Potterhanworth, Lincolnshire
Printed in Great Britain by Ashford Colour Press Ltd, Gosport, Hampshire

*Inter-Varsity Press publishes Christian books that are true to the Bible and that
communicate the gospel, develop discipleship and strengthen the church for its mission
in the world.*

*Inter-Varsity Press is closely linked with the Universities and Colleges Christian
Fellowship, a student movement connecting Christian Unions in universities and colleges
throughout Great Britain, and a member movement of the International Fellowship of
Evangelical Students. Website: www.uccf.org.uk*

Contents

Foreword

My friends will note the irony of me writing the foreword to a book on technology. I just missed out on the computer age during my education and have been unable (some would say unwilling) to catch up ever since. But however old we are, and whether we are technophiles or technophobes, we are all deeply impacted by the digital revolution, for good and ill. Technology is no longer just a part of life in which we can choose to participate or not, but rather it shapes the context in which we all live. We can too easily be swept along by the pace of change and all that comes with it, without pausing to reflect on what is happening to us as a result, and whether we should accept, approve or resist it. This excellent book provides us with a much-needed opportunity to consider how we should engage as Christians with these new realities.

I first met Ed and Pete, the authors, when they were young rugby-playing students, just starting out in the Christian life. They have since lost a lot of muscle, but have grown in other ways, which make them ideal guides through this terrain. They know their way round the world of Google, Facebook and Twitter, but, most importantly, they recognize that the map and compass we need to navigate well in the digital age are found in the ancient words of the Bible, which remains God's living word today.

Ed and Pete help us to see how the story of the advance of technology fits within the backdrop of the big story of the world, as outlined in Scripture, from creation to redemption via the fall. This perspective prevents an unqualified acceptance or rejection of technology, but demands that we respond with both a yes and a no. Those who like simple answers to every question might be frustrated by this approach, but *Virtually Human* has a more ambitious goal. We are not simply told what to do, but rather we are taught principles that will help us assess for ourselves how we should live in a world that still reflects the goodness of God's creation, but is marred by human sin.

Our society is awash with information, which is always readily available just a few clicks away. In that context our greatest need is not more knowledge. Those who read, digest and apply this book will grow in something far more valuable: the true wisdom that fears God, seeks to put him first in all things and brings glory to his name.

Vaughan Roberts
Oxford, October 2015

Acknowledgments

After several months emailing ideas back and forth we realized that if this book was actually going to get written, we would need to set aside the time to sit down and write it. So we camped out at Pete's flat 100 metres from London's Old Street 'Silicon' Roundabout and got to work. Several late nights, plenty of coffee and many bad jokes later, we finally had a draft in passable shape to send to Sam Parkinson at IVP.

Since then we have continued to work hard revising and improving the manuscript, incorporating the excellent feedback from reviewers and building up not a few debts of gratitude along the way.

Thanks are particularly due to Sam Parkinson and the team at IVP for backing us as first-time authors and helping us enormously along the way; to Vaughan Roberts for encouraging us to write this book in the first place; to William Barker, Grant Blank, Andy Geers and an anonymous IVP reviewer for reading through the entire book when it was still an early draft and giving some really helpful feedback; to all those who have invited us to speak on technology and to those who have listened patiently without actually inviting either of us to talk (at length); to Dan Strange for teaching us how to connect Christ and culture, and for looking at the manuscript; lastly to our wives Rebecca and Liubov for enduring long discussions and being helpfully honest when our attempts to be insightful or humorous were just that – attempts. Dear reader, you will never know the pain they have spared you!

To our children. May you flourish in this digital world.

Introduction

A Google product manager recently announced that the company was having to take action to protect the fibre-optic cables that carry digital data under the Pacific Ocean. The cause of concern was as real as it was unlikely: shark attacks! These lines laid across the floor of the ocean are the backbone of the World Wide Web, and if they were to be chewed through, then billions of bytes of data could get lost in the intestines of the Internet! Fortunately we don't need to worry; Google are reinforcing the cables with a material that is stronger than Kevlar. We can all keep surfing the Net safe in the knowledge that Jaws' deep-sea snack won't impact our browsing.

This is a great news story. It is so strange that it has to be true, and it gives us plenty to chew on (apologies). The reason we open with it is that it brings home the physical, down-to-earth reality of the virtual world. The Internet can seem to be 'out there' in the ether, a new dimension of existence beyond the physical. It promises a paradigm shift that can take us beyond the limitations of the old order of things. But when we realize that the digital world is held together by cables dangling precariously between the continents – cables that need to be reinforced so that they don't become shark food – the physicality and the frailty of our brave new world is revealed.

Even Google, the iconic pioneer of the digital age, is having to wrestle with our human inability to control the physical creation. As exciting as the new future seems, many of the old questions about human life in our world still remain for us to answer.

That is why this book is not just for those who avidly read tech magazines like *Wired*. If we think technology, these days we naturally think about smartphones, apps and incredible medical equipment. Perhaps what we think about less is how the technology we have adopted frames the way in which we live. The screens we look into don't only keep us in touch and entertained; they also shape the way we interact with each other and the world. The digital world is designed to update our sense of what is humanly possible and how we can truly flourish. Today, technology is less an aspect of life than the backdrop against which the familiar questions of human life are being played out. As we go on through the book, we will see that while the digital world might seem very new, the questions it raises are in fact timeless:

- Where have we come from and where are we going? (chapter 2)
- How do we make sense of the world we live in? (chapter 3)
- What shapes our deepest identity? (chapter 4)
- What does it mean to cultivate positive and flourishing relationships? (chapter 5)
- How can we find our bearings in a world where time seems to move so quickly? (chapter 6)

- How can we make sense of sex and sexuality? (chapter 7)
- What is true wisdom and where is it found? (chapter 8)

Technology firms know that technology is fundamentally concerned with the nature of human life. That is why their adverts rarely focus on the technology itself. Pete used to work as a marketing consultant for communication and high-tech firms, and their strategy is usually to provide consumers with a vision of human flourishing. We rarely buy new technology simply because of what it can do – the speed of the processor or size of the memory. We invest in technology because we believe that what it can do enables us to live life better.

A matter of perspective

In this book we will be looking at how technology is re-imagining some of the answers to these 'big questions' of life. In fact we believe that technology is such an embedded part of modern life that it is nearly impossible to consider these questions without considering technology's impact. So whether you are a technophile, technophobe, or most likely somewhere in between, our hope is that this book will have lots to say to you, giving you a vision of life that will help you to flourish in our digital world.

In exploring this transforming vision the challenge we will face is one of perspective. As we will often observe, there is a popular and compelling story about our digital world. But is life in the story as good as we feel it should be? Is the story true?

Whether you are aware of it or not, you will be familiar with the story. It has been told countless times through adverts, articles and even Olympic opening ceremonies. It goes something like this:

Once upon a time, in the olden days, the world was a very different place and our ancestors lived very different lives. Things were much more brutal back then. *Homo sapiens* had evolved into existence, but in those days people were really still in beta testing – an earlier, more primitive form of the species – maybe we could call them HS 1.0.

Over time, and through a series of incredible insights by a handful of people, humankind grew up from infancy to an enlightened state of maturity. We learned how to govern ourselves with justice and equity, living in newfound freedom from the constraints of the past. We invented clocks to take control of time and built vast machines to produce what we needed more efficiently. We printed great books to read, and designed new modes of transport so we could travel and take our new life of liberty around the world.

Then came the Internet, and humanity entered a new age of HS 2.0 where the vision of peace and liberty could at last be fully realized. The strict hierarchies of the world were stripped away, and a new pattern of life was established where time and space are not the barriers they used to be. Now everyone is able to connect. We have moved from prehistory to history to hyper-history and isn't it *amazing*!

We have told the story tongue in cheek, to provoke you to think. But please do not assume that because of this we are cynics about technology. The truth is we love technology and see it as a good gift from a loving God. We do think our digital world is amazing.

But we also want to be realistic. There are plenty of dissenting voices – authors, newspaper editors, parents, teachers, academics – all casting doubt on the goodness and the truth of the story of the digital world that ends in the utopia of hyper-history.

They argue that the technology that seems to promise so much is damaging our relationships, our ability to concentrate, our public life, our children. The fear is that we are becoming distracted, addicted, disorientated, not more but less truly human.

With every new technology there is a new wave of techno-scepticism, alerting us to what author Andrew Keen refers to as #digitalvertigo. Maybe some of these concerns are expressed by the nagging voice you hear within: is this new digital world really so good? Maybe the story that has digital connectivity as the pinnacle of humanity is as much 'hype' as it is 'hyper'.

God's vantage point

So which is it? The story of progress or the voice of concern? The chances are that you are reading this book because you are aware that the answer is neither a stubborn resistance to technology just because it is new, nor a naive must-have mentality where every upgrade is essential. But where does that leave us, other than heading to our favourite search engine for some advice? One of the great virtues of this digital age is that we have the privilege of access to so many other viewpoints. These can help us reflect on our own perspective, but we also face a navigation challenge. How do we find our way through so many different opinions and stories to discover where genuine truth and goodness are to be found?

The philosopher Charles Taylor talks of the 'cross pressures' that we feel in the late-modern world. We are caught, he argues, between conflicting points of view and multiple ways of life and belief.[1] Through the Internet, different ideas come at us thick and fast. We are constantly exposed to opinions that are incompatible with our own but seem to have significant support. We want to be even-handed and consider other understandings, but how do we evaluate them? Just as importantly, how do we assess our own beliefs? Do we just bounce back and forth between opposing views like the ball in that classic 2D video game *Pong*?

We can appeal to our own culture or tradition, but then, with many other cultures mediated to us through the Internet, on what grounds can we say our culture is right and another is wrong? We can resort to a type of personal subjectivity where every statement begins, 'I think . . .' or, 'It seems to me . . .' But in a digital world where every person can have his or her own blog, the retreat to individual relativism (all opinions are equally valid) just throws more balls into the *Pong* game. Life becomes even more confusing.

What we need is some perspective. A vantage point that helps us reflect on the big and important questions that technology is posing. A perspective that frees us from our own cultural short-sightedness. At this point we ourselves need to come clean: we do not have that perspective! (Sorry if this is news to you.) But, if we can be so bold, neither do you! If you think about it, for a person to have perfect vision of the world, he or she must be outside creation. Consequently, this perfect perspective belongs uniquely to God.

As the Creator, God is distinct from his creation without being distant from it. He is not biased or bound to a particular culture. He discerns perfectly what is good, and what isn't, in each and every time and place. The digital age is no exception. Technology has not taken him by surprise. God knows the good in technology because its goodness comes from him. It is the goodness of creation that he always intended to be taken up and developed by humankind, as they filled the earth with his image. And he knows fully the harm technology can do if it is taken and used against him and against other people.

God understands us and our world perfectly. What is more, he doesn't just know the world from a distance. He is also the Creator who 'became flesh' in Jesus Christ. Through Jesus Christ we can see the world as God sees it and be reconciled to live in it in relationship with him. Through listening to what God has to say in the Bible, through embracing the frame of life he gives us, through coming to know Jesus Christ who is at the heart of God's story, God gives us the perspective we need to flourish.

This idea might well seem strange to you. But 'What does the Bible have to say about technology?' is a question we are asked frequently. Remember, the questions technology poses are not simply technological questions. They are questions about a vision for human life. They are questions about how to live life well, how to understand ourselves and how to interact with others. These questions are the questions that the Bible does answer, and its answers are found in a person: Jesus Christ. Jesus may not have used Twitter, browsed the Internet or written a blog, but his teaching, his life and his work are central to enabling us to navigate our digital world.

If you aren't familiar with the Bible you might be surprised at Jesus' answers – they aren't what you would expect. In fact, the Bible's answers are surprising to most Christians too. Sometimes they will challenge deeply held convictions. At other times they will expose blind spots. It may be that there will be things we have to stop doing, and in other areas we may have to start something. What is for certain is that if we as authors do our task well, and if you are open to change, then by the end of this book you won't see technology in quite the same way. In fact, we hope you won't see yourself, God or his world in quite the same way either.

The way of digital flourishing

The book is split into two parts. Part 1 (chapters 1 to 3) seeks to provide a framework to engage with the digital world. Part 2 (chapters 4 to 8) develops this framework in relation to different areas of life. We don't think that part 2 deals with all the issues our digital world is facing, nor does it even cover all of the major digital information technologies. Our hope is that by considering some of the important technologies and the issues they raise, you will grasp the framework and be able to apply it yourself. We hope to enable you to reflect and develop life-practices to better navigate the fast-changing landscape of our digital world. Here is a taste of what is to come . . .

In part 1:

- Chapter 1 considers the nature of technology. Is it 'Just a tool?' Is technology a collection of sometimes scary, often cool, but essentially value-neutral tools that we can just pick up and put down? Or is it something with a deeper, more substantial impact on us?
- Chapter 2 asks the question: 'What's the story?' We consider how all technology comes to us with a story. It presents to us a vision of human flourishing. But is it the right story, and if not, how do we retell the story without simply tearing up the manuscript?
- Chapter 3 is called 'The interface'. Here we set out a 'yes' and 'no' approach to technology that both affirms the inherent goodness of technology and also challenges the sin and idolatry that is in technology as much as it is in any area of human life. This 'yes' and 'no' dynamic (known as 'subversive fulfilment') is not about seeking a 'Goldilocks' middle ground, but points

instead to the fulfilment of the hopes of technology by challenging and redeeming its failures.

In part 2, the 'yes and no' framework is applied to different aspects of life in the digital world:

- Chapter 4, 'I tweet therefore I am', considers the question of human identity and how digital technologies enable us to reimagine and recreate who we are.
- Chapter 5, 'The social network', considers the way the structure of the Internet shapes our relationships. We examine the consequences – good and bad – of living online.
- Chapter 6, 'Real time', reflects on technology's impact on our perception of time. Is life really getting faster and faster? What does it mean to 'make the best use of time' today?
- Chapter 7, 'Virtual sex', considers the story of freedom that accompanies the modern Western view of sex. We explore the nature of our newfound sexual freedom and ask why this 'freedom' is also causing fragmentation and constraint.
- Chapter 8, 'Searching for knowledge', is about how the Internet has influenced our view of knowledge. We discuss the benefits of online search engines and consider the pitfalls of this new way to know. In an age of information overload we explore the aim of knowing and the importance of wisdom.

Finally the conclusion draws together reflections and key areas for personal change, as well as hitting 'refresh' on the framework we have been using throughout. Our hope is that this enables you to continue to reflect on your engagement with technology, develop helpful practices in our digital world, and help others to do the same.

Throughout the book, we are aware of the challenge posed by seeking to reflect on our digital world in 'real time'. Even if we wanted to, we can't log off from the world, retreat from technology, do our thinking and then re-emerge ready to engage. We all live within the story of the digital age; in fact we are involved in writing the story. But the fact that we cannot step out of the world should not worry us. God sent his Son into the world, writing himself into the world's history and engaging from within. Jesus lived in the world without being conformed to it. As we look to him, and follow him, there is the possibility of a renewed, God-honouring and deeply satisfying way of life in this as in every age.

Part 1

I

Just a tool?

Have you ever held off investing in a new technology only to find that it was far better than you had thought it would be? Or ever considered the apps that you would not want to be without? Have you ever felt your smartphone has got in the way of a conversation? Or ever wondered how people manage to stay on the pavement when they never look up from their Snapchat feed? Have you ever marvelled at the way Google maps can help you get exactly where you want to be when you are lost in a city you have never visited before? Have you ever felt a bit too attached to your email? Or wondered whether Facebook is strengthening or weakening your friendships? Have you ever received a message that cheered you up when you felt alone? Or heard from a friend you had lost touch with after he or she found you online?

Life in our digital world is full of these contradictions. If we take time to reflect, it is impossible to be utterly negative or utterly positive about technology. But all these questions raise two more: whom should we thank for the benefits of the technology that we enjoy? And whom should we blame for the bugs?

Different books on technology assign the responsibility in different ways. One common approach focuses on the users. Technology is neutral, this line argues; the heroes or villains in the story are the people involved. We can use technology for great good and great evil. If we get it right we should feel proud, and if we get it wrong we must take the blame.

A second group pushes back. They say this first position doesn't take account of the power of technology. We are constrained by the way technology is designed. We have no choice but to use it in a certain way. If Facebook leaves us lonely it is a fault with the network, or the technology on which it relies.

If the first approach assigns the responsibility to the users, this second approach casts us as passive recipients determined by technological powers beyond our control. We might thank the designers, or blame them, but the responsibility for the way technology is shaping our lives is largely out of our hands.

Which group is right? To us, neither position seems to capture the reality of what is going on. If we want to get to the bottom of what it means to live well in this world of technology, we are going to have to dive into this debate and consider what technology actually is. Specifically we need to ask: is technology just a tool? Is it neutral?

Now, this clearly isn't the only book exploring the nature of technology and how it is shaping our lives. This is a hot topic with an abundance of books and blog posts devoted to it. But there are two important features of our approach that are distinct from what you might find elsewhere. First, we are committed to going beyond the polarization between pro- and anti-technology voices that is a feature of much current discussion. Facebook, for example, is neither wholly good nor wholly bad. But if that is the case, how should we approach how we interact with it? Our decisions rest on discernment, which means we need to understand how the blessing and the bugs of technology are related. The second distinctive feature of the approach in this book is that we are committed to engaging with technology in the world under God. If it seems unnecessary or counter-intuitive to bring God into the story of technology, we hope it won't as you read on.

This may well seem counter-intuitive to you. At one time it was widely believed that progress in science and technology made belief in God irrelevant, if not irrational. We still breathe this cultural air. However, more recently the 'God is dead' story of secularism has had to be retracted. Technology simply hasn't consigned questions of spirituality and belief in God to history. How could it when technology is often seeking to frame answers to the 'big questions' of life? Questions that deal with the existence and nature of God. Purely secular understandings of technology are therefore bound to be limited.

So our approach is not secular – that is already clear – but neither is it vaguely spiritual. To take God seriously as God, his place in the conversation must be at the beginning. What other place can we assign to the Author of creation? What is more, we believe that the God of creation is the God who took flesh in Jesus Christ (John 1:14) and is now present by the Holy Spirit (John 14:16–17). With Christians through the last two millennia we believe that he has revealed his will in the Scriptures given to the church (2 Timothy 3:16). We won't be defending these beliefs here since there are plenty of other good books that do that.[1] Instead, we will be taking this Christian understanding as our foundational assumption. Our aim is to show how a Christian understanding of the world makes sense of technology, and how a Christian approach to technology can lead us to flourish in our digital world.

At times our Christian convictions will be more explicit than at others, but they are informing our thinking throughout. We begin in this chapter by raising some essential questions about the nature of technology and how it operates in society. If you read this wanting more explicitly Christian content then be patient; it is coming. Later chapters actively seek to bring our understanding of technology within the Christian story of life in the world. If you read those scratching your head and asking what Jesus has to do with smartphones or social media, we hope you will be persuaded as the book goes on that the answer is, 'everything'.

Digging a bit deeper

Imagine I am out for a romantic meal with my wife. We are at our favourite restaurant, having a dinner date together for the first time in a few weeks. As we sit down, I take my iPhone out of my pocket and put it on the table. I just place it there. I don't refer to it. I don't use it. It's just there. Now let's ask the question again: is it neutral? Of course not! Putting the phone on the table has reshaped the environment. Even if she says nothing, my wife is now thinking: 'Why did he take his phone out? Is he expecting a call? Does he want to check his messages? Doesn't he want to speak to me? Is his phone more interesting to him than I am?'

Martin Heidegger was a famous German philosopher in the twentieth century who thought deeply about technology. He was convinced that technology was not neutral, and to back up his point he used an illustration about mining (his name sounds like 'digger', so it's a memorable example).

Heidegger's point was that once we have the technology of mining, we view every field in a different way, as a possible mine. We approach the field with the question: what resources might be buried underneath it? Could we mine it? Would it be better to mine it or leave it as a field?

The point of both illustrations is this: it seems counter-intuitive, but the essence of technology is, in fact, not anything technological. In a deep sense, technology is not simply about microchips and fibre-optics and lines of computer code. Technology is like a frame through which we see the world, which then becomes the world in which we live.

'The digger' is a pretty deep thinker(!) and he says lots of other things, some of which are more helpful than others. If we learn this one thing from him, we will have learnt well: technology is not neutral.

> Everywhere we remain unfree and chained to technology,
> whether we passionately affirm or deny it. But we are
> delivered over to it in the worst possible way when we regard
> it as something neutral; for this conception . . . makes us
> utterly blind to the essence of technology.[2]

This may seem like an overstatement. Surely I'm not chained to technology! But think carefully for a moment. What he is saying is that if we are unconscious about the way that technology frames the world, if we are unthinking about its real impact on us and think of it as 'just a tool', then isn't there an important sense in which we are blind to its true power? Think of the way even everyday words have been changed by technology: web, friend, surfing, like, blackberry, connect, search, refresh, text, feed, status (to mention a few). Changing terms that millions of people use every day is a quite remarkable manifestation of power. It is even more powerful when it is done and few of us notice!

Just a tool?

English satirist and broadcaster Charlie Brooker is someone

we might expect to be a firm techno-sceptic. He is the author of a dystopian television series, *Black Mirror*, which explores (sparing few sensibilities) the impact of technology on life in the modern world. But Brooker is no technophobe. He, and his actors, are obsessed with their 'black mirrors':

> The show isn't anti-technology. I'm quite techno and gadgety. I hope that the stories demonstrate that it's not a technological problem we have. It's a human one. Human frailties are maybe amplified by it. Technology is a tool that has allowed us to swipe around like an angry toddler.[3]

'Technology is a tool.' What problems there are with technology are problems with the people using it. That sounds pretty plausible. Plausible enough, in fact, to have acquired a large number of followers and been given a name: 'instrumentalism'. Sir Tim Berners-Lee is credited as the person who invented the World Wide Web. In an interview in 2005, fifteen years after his groundbreaking work in a Genevan science laboratory, he was asked to evaluate the achievement of his invention. His response reveals his hopes for the future as well as his own understanding, which is a good example of the 'instrumentalist' approach:

> It's a new medium, it's a universal medium and it's not itself a medium which inherently makes people do good things, or bad things. It allows people to do what they want to do more efficiently. It allows people to exist in an information space which doesn't know geographical boundaries. My hope is that it'll be very positive in bringing people together around the planet, because it'll make communication between different countries more possible.[4]

If we are inclined to agree with Charlie Brooker and Sir Tim Berners-Lee, that isn't surprising; there is surely something to the instrumentalist argument that is attractive. Even though it can appear to be pretty down on people as the cause of the problems, it is a kind of pessimism that hides a deeper optimism under the surface. If people are the problem, people can be the solution too. After all, on this view, we are the ones in control.

Isn't this very biblical too? The Bible is quite clear that we are on shaky ground when we start to think of problems in the world as 'out there'. We human beings make and use technology, so don't any problems ultimately come back to us? Well yes, but before we go too far with this view, we need to be careful lest we forget our German lesson: we may not be neutral, but technology isn't neutral either.

Those who oppose the 'technology is a tool' understanding often point to the way technology seems to be the driving force in changing society. Think about how Facebook is changing the way we relate, or how Internet browsing is influencing our attention span, or how instant messaging has meant we talk less on the phone, or how Twitter is feeding our appetite for instant news updates.

'The medium is the message' said Marshall McLuhan, arguing that the way in which communication takes place changes the content of the message. The different forms of media, in other words, are not just passive tools; they themselves carry a depth of meaning that shapes society. Neil Postman is a student of McLuhan who takes on this understanding in his book, *Amusing Ourselves to Death*. He argues that cultural decline in the second half of the twentieth century was due to the decline of the 'Age of Typography' and the ascendance of the 'Age of Television':

> This change-over has dramatically and irreversibly shifted the content and meaning of public discourse, since two media so vastly different cannot accommodate the same ideas. As the influence of print wanes, the content of politics, religion, education, and anything else that comprises public business must change and be recast in terms that are most suitable to television.[5]

This understanding of technology, underlining the importance of the means of communication, also seems plausible. It too has its own name: 'technological determinism'.

This seems to have important biblical grounding as well. We would not expect technology to be value neutral, because God has not made the world value neutral. In the opening chapter of Genesis (even before human beings are created) we are told six times that 'God saw that it was good' (1:4, 10, 12, 18, 21, 25). One view that is prevalent in technology is that the material in the world is neutral and we give it value by our creative activity. But if the world is ingrained with value from the moment of its creation, then it is little wonder that technology is not neutral either.

So which is right: instrumentalism (technology is just a tool) or determinism (technology is in the driving seat)?

Surely both contain important points that we need to take on board. The technologies we adopt are made by groups of people with goals in mind. They are aiming to achieve certain ends: to make life quicker, cheaper, more relationally connected. So there is a 'tool-like' function to technology. The Internet was the result of the US military's need for a communications network that could withstand nuclear attack in the Cold War. The Google search engine was developed as a more fruitful way of finding useful information from the Web. Facebook was intended to connect students at Harvard.

The World Wide Web itself was designed by Sir Tim Berners-Lee as a way of sharing research findings among nuclear physicists. So Nicholas Carr writes, 'Every technology is an expression of human will. Through our tools, we seek to expand our power and control over our circumstances – over nature, over time and distance, over one another.' He adds, 'It certainly appears that, as the instrumentalists claim, our tools are firmly under our control.'[6]

But, as Carr goes on to point out, the determinist case is also persuasive. We surely do seek to assert our will on the world through technology, but aren't we already constrained by the technological world in which we live? And once we start using these 'tools' we have designed, don't they inevitably shape us and the way we see the world?

> Though we're rarely conscious of the fact, many of the routines of our lives follow paths laid down by technologies that came into use long before we were born. It's an overstatement to say that technology progresses autonomously – our adoption and use of tools are heavily influenced by economic, political, and demographic considerations – but it isn't an overstatement to say that progress has its own logic, which is not always consistent with the intentions or wishes of the toolmakers and tool users. Sometimes our tools do what we tell them to. Other times, we adapt ourselves to our tools' requirements.[7]

We like to think that we are in control of the world, but we are aware that so often we are not. It is empowering to imagine we are riding through the world towards a horizon we choose for ourselves, creating technology to serve our own vision of life. The reality is often closer to the observation made by Ralph Waldo Emerson: 'Things are in the saddle / And ride mankind.'[8]

As we go through this book we need to remember both these insights. First, technology is not just a tool; it changes the way we view the world and profoundly impacts us, often in ways we are not fully aware of. But second, we need to take responsibility as the architects and 'users' of technology for the ways we use it in God's world.

All technology tells a story

A large part of technology's appeal is the story of life that modern technology brings with it. The most successful gadgets, websites and apps are the ones that persuade us of our need for them by showing us the life of blessing that they make possible. Look at the ads – they don't major so much on technical specifications as on giving a vision of human flourishing where the product is the crucial component. It is the way in which the latest iPad can empower you to interact with the world and shape reality that is its selling point. For Apple, in particular, the beauty of design is intended to mirror the power of the creative harmony its products can bring to your life.

On the surface, each advert and each new technology of the digital age has its own story. Under the surface, the stories have a unity in the story of freedom that belongs to the late-modern world. The message is that whoever you are, wherever you come from, you alone define yourself, you alone write the script that you will follow through life. You are free (as the Nike slogan goes) to 'write the future'. Steve Jobs summed it up in his speech to the graduating class at Stanford University in 2005:

> Your time is limited, so don't waste it living someone else's life. Don't be trapped by dogma – which is living with the results

of other people's thinking. Don't let the noise of others' opinions drown out your own inner voice. And most important, have the courage to follow your heart and intuition. They somehow already know what you truly want to become. Everything else is secondary.[9]

This is the appeal of the digital world: there is no story pre-written; rather, with the power of technology, we can all code our own. The thing is (and we're not just trying to be clever here) that the 'life is a blank-page story' is, of course, itself a story. We could call it the 'no-story story'. It doesn't sound too interesting when put like that. But it is amazing how it has captured our cultural imagination!

'Everyone can publish, and broadcast, and create; we just need to follow our heart.' One of our aims in this book is to pull back the curtain on this story. We will find much good that we will want to affirm. We will also need to raise some important questions. The best bits of this story, we will see, are actually part of a greater story of life.

A story of humanity

Finally, a really important thing for us to notice as we start to explore the story of life in the digital world is that it is a story about humanity. People are the central characters, and the gadgets of technology play a part only so far as they promise to improve or threaten to challenge our story.

The key issue is not so much, 'What can technology do?' as, 'What can technology do *for us*?' As with all the big stories of life, questions about who we are as human beings, and who we are becoming, lie right at the heart of things.

Nick Bostrom is Professor of Philosophy at Oxford University and Director of the Future of Humanity Institute.

According to Bostrom, the story of the digital age is the story of human beings going beyond the limits of their biological nature. It finds its beginnings in the development of modern science and the insight that science could be used to augment and extend human life. As early as the eighteenth century, French philosopher and mathematician, Nicolas de Condorcet, was asking the question:

> Would it be absurd now to suppose that the improvement of the human race should be regarded as capable of unlimited progress? That a time will come when death would result only from extraordinary accidents or the more and more gradual wearing out of vitality, and that, finally, the duration of the average interval between birth and wearing out has itself no specific limit whatsoever? No doubt man will not become immortal, but cannot the span constantly increase between the moment he begins to live and the time when naturally, without illness or accident, he finds life a burden?[10]

Through the nineteenth and twentieth centuries, technological developments have given these questions a new plausibility. Bostrom and others have taken them up in a movement called 'transhumanism'. According to Bostrom,

> Transhumanists emphasize the enormous potential for genuine improvements in human well-being and human flourishing that are attainable only via technological transformation . . . we could realize great values by venturing beyond our current biological limitations.[11]

Imagine for example (says the transhumanist) the future possibilities of gene therapy. Every human ill that can be traced back to our genes, from obesity to low IQ, from cancer to weak joints, could be eradicated. Every baby could be screened and then all the 'faulty' genes corrected – each human being would be perfect from conception. (Perhaps you recognize the story? It has been taken up by more than a few sci-fi films as the basis for their plot.)

The future is new, but the story isn't. The transhumanist tale is merely the latest version of a story told many times throughout the history of the modern world. In fact, there have been no fewer than three Humanist Manifestos (1933, 1973, 2003), each fuelled by advances in science and technology and each promising things like:

> Using technology wisely, we can control our environment, conquer poverty, markedly reduce disease, extend our life-span, significantly modify our behavior, alter the course of human evolution and cultural development, unlock vast new powers, and provide humankind with unparalleled opportunity for achieving an abundant and meaningful life. (Humanist Manifesto II)

This was written in 1973, but doesn't it sound contemporary? To reflect on what really happened in history and the way that each manifesto has been pretty brutally exposed is to give a helpful check on the techno-optimism that has continued within the transhumanist vision.

Please don't get us wrong here. We aren't countering techno-optimism with techno-pessimism. Nor are we denying many of the incredible ways human life has been enriched as a result of modern science and technology.

Our awareness of history should not leave us pessimistic about the future and technology's part in it; far from it. But we do need to be clear that the transhuman dream of technological progress towards a fast-approaching utopia is just that – a dream. And as with all utopian dreams, there is no clear way of ensuring it doesn't turn into a dystopian nightmare.

Rewiring the system

There are two dangers that we are seeking to avoid in our approach to technology in this book. There is so much that is good in the digital world and much that we enjoy and are thankful for. But we don't want to be blind to the reality that the world of modern technology is not all good.

On the one hand, we need to avoid being uncritically positive. On the other hand, we need to be careful not to react too quickly against the way technology is implicated in the darker aspects of life in the digital world.

So are we looking for a Goldilocks midpoint then? A response to technology that is not too hot and not too cold? Well, not that either. Trying to stand at the midpoint between two wrong answers results in the kind of discomfort you might have experienced if you are not a trained gymnast and have ever tried to do the splits.

The approach we will take is the approach that lines up with our theology. The technical term for it is 'subversive fulfilment' and it was taught to us by a subversive theologian of culture called Dan Strange. Our aim is to enter into the story of modern technology, seeking to explore where it has come from and what it reveals about life in the world. As we do this we will be able to affirm much that is good and true, but we will also see humankind's sinful distortion of the true good that comes from God.

Technology does play an important part in the story of life, and the story of life does feature humanity at its heart. But our story is not a blank page. Our role brings with it great freedom to design and create and flourish, but we are not the authors of life.

So far as we try to make use of technology within a story that asserts our ownership and our control of the world, it will eventually fail us. Modern technology cannot deliver life because it is not God. As we will see in the next chapter, the digital world needs to be rewired within his story.

Questions

1. What role does God play in the way you engage with technology? Why?
2. Have a look at these two videos (watch them a couple of times): 'The Things That Connect Us' (Facebook) and 'Social Media Guard' (Coke). What stories about technology are they telling? Which do you think is a better portrayal of life in the digital world? Why?
3. 'The essence of technology is by no means anything technological' (Martin Heidegger). What do you think this means? What are the implications for how we view digital technology?
4. It is common to view technology as a neutral tool. Can you recognize where you have come across this approach? What is wrong with it?
5. What is the problem with a binary approach to technology that considers it to be completely positive or negative?

2

What's the story?

The power of technology is the power of the future. At its best, technology seems to promise a better world where many of the deepest problems of the present have been overcome. Science fiction writers have found rich pickings in these futures. But some of their visions, it has to be said, are more compelling than others.

In 2014, *Time Out* magazine ran an article listing 'The ten sci-fi movie inventions we wish were real'. In first place, above the car from *Back to the Future*, and the electromagnetic shrink-ray from *Honey, I Shrunk the Kids*, was the 'translation collar' from the Pixar animation *Up*. This revolutionary invention holds out the promise that dog owners need no longer be in the dark about the deepest thoughts of their canine companions. Nothing so practical as helping us communicate with people who don't speak our language, the 'translation collar' turns the thoughts (such as they are) of Dug the dog into speech![1]

There are of course many more down-to-earth examples of the way technology has brought what seemed to be an unthinkable future into the lived reality of the present. Consider how travel has been transformed in the last hundred years, or medical care, or communications, or education. Twenty years ago the idea of video calling over the Internet using a device you could carry in your pocket would have been a dream. Thirty years ago the idea of seeing a scan of your unborn baby on a digital monitor and taking home a photo to stick on the fridge would have been unthinkable. Part of the wonder of modern technology is that it has solved so many problems of life. It has brought incredible, and rapid, progress.

The aim of this chapter is to consider this story of progress and ask some questions about what drives it and where it is heading. In order to do that, however, we are going to need to take a step back and examine what we usually take for granted. The story of technological optimism is ingrained in the way we live, such that we are conditioned to assume that every innovation is an improvement. We don't need to think too much about it; we simply have to 'click here for updates to take effect'.

But is it right that we experience every upgrade as the very word tells us we must? There are an increasing number of sceptics when it comes to the kind of progress story that technology is designed to tell. Many Christians are among them, looking back to a time in Western history when the church was more prominent in society, and the values of the culture seemed more biblical. However, while there is much to learn from history, from people and periods where God's Word was more widely honoured and applied, to pin our hopes on the past instead of the future is an implausible as well as impossible answer to the ambiguities of technology. Implausible since it assumes that the past was free of the problems of the present. Even if it was, the past had plenty of problems of its own. Impossible since we are unable to turn back the clock. We live in God's world and in his time. He has given us life in the present and calls us not to live in the past, but to learn from the past for the sake of the present and the future. This word of biblical wisdom is one we need to keep in mind: 'Say not "Why were the former days better than these?" For it is not from wisdom that you ask this' (Ecclesiastes 7:10).

Rather than accepting technology's imaginary story of the future or reacting against it with a story of the past, we need a better story that connects the past and the future. A story that doesn't reject progress but redefines it in a way that is true to the reality of life, a story that enables us to discern the real way 'forward' in an age of constant upgrades.

The shape of progress

Let's go back to the progress story. In 1994, those in the market for a smartphone had only one choice. The IBM Simon was the first smartphone and he wasn't exactly slim, weighing in at half a kilogram. His battery lasted an hour and he cost $899 (nearly £600). Perhaps not surprisingly, a smartphone that was so heavy it was likely to rip a hole in your pocket was not too successful.

Consider now the release of the iPhone 6. One of the key marketing points for the iPhone 6 was its size. 'It is quite like the old iPhone, but it is bigger,' Pete can remember an Apple store 'genius' telling him excitedly. If you had asked someone at the time of its launch 'Is the iPhone 6 better than the iPhone 5?' he or she might have looked at you as if you were stupid. 'Of course the 6 is better than the 5 . . . if it was worse, it would be called a 4!'

Progressive numbering creates the appearance of progress. But is it actually progress? Not so long ago progress in phones was all about them being smaller. Now is it better because it is bigger? We can hear Simon the original smartphone's confusion. He was criticized for a fault we now consider a virtue!

Of course we understand that the iPhone's size relates to its screen and not its overall bulk, but this example begins to draw out the question of what constitutes progress. Haven't you ever wondered whether the 'new software update with bug fixes' is just fixing bugs the old one created? Have you ever been frustrated that the latest system upgrade actually slows your computer down? Is every upgrade really an improvement? Adding a higher number to a name may give the appearance of things having advanced, but what actually is improvement? What does it mean to progress?

Why not pause for a moment and reflect on the last product or upgrade that you felt was a 'must have'. Why was it so important to you? What was the promise made to you in its marketing (implied or explicit)? Did it deliver on its promise?

Pete remembers updating to iCloud Beta apps because of 'important new functionality'. But then he found he could no longer open his old Pages documents with Beta. Beta was better – a bit – but in many other ways it was worse. The problem was, once he'd upgraded he couldn't go back. It was like a ratchet effect. Such is the way of progress!

Don't get us wrong here. We aren't denying that technology updates sometimes do improve things. The big screen of the iPhone 6 definitely made it better to watch videos and surf the Net and type. What we want to challenge is the constant-upgrade script that technology seems to make us live by. It seems to be in the technological air we breathe these days that upgrading will deliver human flourishing all by itself. But is it delivering? The point we are driving at is this one: progress can't be progress without a direction and destination.

C. S. Lewis famously commented,

> Progress means getting nearer to the place you want to be. And if you have taken a wrong turning, then to go forward does not get you any nearer. If you are on the wrong road, progress means doing an about-turn and walking back to the right road; and in that case the man who turns back soonest is the most progressive man.[2]

We need to reflect on what we might call the 'modern assumption of progress'. This assumption is at the heart of the story of the modern world. As a human race we often think we are on the straight road of improvement (with the occasional bump, but nothing we can't overcome!). Signposts to 'The Future' line the way with the promise that the destination is getting closer all the time. And we only need look in the rear-view mirror to see how far we have come. We are getting closer and closer to the goal. But pause for a moment. What goal are we actually heading for? What is 'The Future' we are going towards? Are we really heading in the right direction?

The reason this is so important is that many of our key decisions about technology are based on an assumption about the goal. Alisdair MacIntyre points this out in his book *After Virtue* where he argues that ethics always presupposes an accepted understanding of what the goal of the good life is.[3] Even if we never actively think about it, life is always heading somewhere. There is no road to nowhere.

So before we get to the part of this book where we start thinking about specific technologies, we need first to understand where we are heading and see the bigger story.

In the beginning

In the 1970s, there was an explosion of innovations in computing. In 1975 the Altair 8800 was on the front cover of the January edition of *Popular Electronics*. It was the first personal computer and unexpectedly the Altair sold thousands. A group of innovators at the vanguard of this new digital age, including key figures such as Bill Gates (Microsoft) and Steve Wozniak (Apple), gathered together under the title 'The Homebrew Club'. One historian of this time comments,

> The club was a hybrid of elements from the radical student movement, the Berkeley community computing activists and electronic hobbyists. Hippy groups in California had been quick to recognize the computer as a device of empowerment. As early as 1972 a group called the People's Computer Company published an impassioned call on the pencil-drawn cover of its first newsletter: 'Computers are mostly used against people instead of for people, used to control people instead of to free them; Time to change all that – we need a . . . People's Computer Company.'[4]

This extended quote captures the mood at the time. There was a heady mix of idealism and innovation, creativity and community. It was the beginning of the digital age and a story that is still unfolding today.

It is a great story with some incredible characters: Ada Lovelace, Alan Turing, Vannevar Bush, Grace Hopper, Larry Roberts, Alan Kay, Steve Jobs, Bill Gates, Tim Berners-Lee, Larry Page, Sergey Brin . . . we could go on and on. Some of the names are famous and some are not. But the story is bigger than any of them. It is a story of incredible collaboration where no problem is beyond a collective solution and where everyone is invited to play a part. We can be involved. That is the promise and the attraction of the story that has become the story of our age.

As inspiring as this story is, of course it can't be the story that frames reality. After all, it only began in the last century or two, and it has only really got going in its present form in the last fifty years. In order to make sense of it we need to place the digital age back in its wider narrative.

The great story we are all in is God's story. It starts not with human ingenuity or innovation but with God and an explosion of his creativity, power and love. 'In the beginning, God created the heavens and the earth' (Genesis 1:1). These may be ancient words, but they pulse with significance.

God spoke, and what he spoke came into being: a universe of incredible possibility and beauty, a world of meaning and value. And what a world it is – no wonder that when the creation is finished, God sees it as 'very good' (Genesis 1:31).

We must recapture this first chapter of the story, because it reframes technology in light of where things really start. As we have been saying, much technological innovation sees the world as a 'blank page' on which the pen of technology can write the future. But the Bible tells us that creation is not blank. It is packed full with meaning and value, structure and beauty. Just as there may be many things a carpenter can make from a piece of wood, if he or she works with the grain to avoid splintering and fraying, so technical innovation must work with the grain of creation. Too often we employ technology to chisel out our own agenda instead, only for it to become cracked and splintered. Creation does not come to us formless, for us to impose on it our technological will. It comes ingrained with value, meaning and orderliness right down to the subatomic level. Technology, rightly conceived, respects the grain of the world as the structure of the freedom God has given to us to innovate within.

At the heart of creation, in organic relationship with the rest of reality, stands the pinnacle of God's design. Of all that God creates, he has no greater innovation than humanity. In Genesis 1:26 the rhythm of the narrative slows down as if to emphasize the importance of what is to come. There is a royal pause, followed by a declaration: 'Let us make man in our image, after our likeness . . . So God created man in his own image, in the image of God he created him; male and female he created them' (Genesis 1:26–27). Bearing God's image, man and woman were also given God's purpose for life in his creation: 'Be fruitful and multiply and fill the earth and subdue it' (Genesis 1:28).

This creation purpose is key to our understanding of technology and its place in God's story of human life. First, it helps us understand where our technological impulse comes from. It does not originate, as is sometimes argued, with a human urge to dominate. Technology does not originally follow the pattern of Prometheus, the character in Greek mythology who stole fire from Mount Olympus to benefit humanity and outwit Zeus. Prometheus has become a symbol for humanity's desire to fight against God while seeking to become like God. Technology can be used in that way but it shouldn't be. Nor is it humanity's way to construct meaning in a meaningless universe. We are technological beings who see the world in different ways and conceive of new possibilities because we are made in the image of God the Creator. As the early Christian thinker Augustine wrote,

> There are many great arts invented and exercised by
> human ingenuity . . . The mind and reason of man shows
> great excellence in contriving such things . . . and is not

this excellence evidence of a great good which man has in his nature?[5]

This nature is implanted in us by an ingenious God as a window on his glory. Consequently, when we marvel at technological innovation there is a sense in which of course we should wonder at what humanity can create, at the intelligence of men and women. But more deeply we should realize that humanity is the image of a great God. God has implanted in humanity these gifts, impulses and desires, so at a far more profound level, everything that is good in technology reveals God to us. To put it plainly, we should be less captivated with our phones and more captivated with God who makes such technology possible.

Often Christians are more prone to thank God for the flowers than they are for Facebook – but both are windows on God's glory.

Thought Provoking

One immediate and practical application of this is giving thanks. How often do we give thanks to God for technology? Often Christians are more prone to thank God for the flowers than they are for Facebook – but both are windows on God's glory. When was the last time you gave thanks to God for the technology that so richly benefits your life? Do you inherently feel that somehow technology is less a part of God's creation that the flora and fauna? Think again. At root the good in any aspect of creation, technological or otherwise, is a gift of God.

Second, the call to 'Be fruitful and multiply, fill the earth and subdue it' sets history on a trajectory. The world in Genesis may be 'very good' but it is not static. God wants it filled with humanity and he wants humanity to be fruitful and subdue creation. If one part of this creation mandate speaks of population increase and procreation, the other part talks of culture forming – agriculture, the economy, the arts and technology (to mention a few areas).

God's work of creation may have been finished, but his plan for creation was not yet complete. The moment he finishes his creative work he orientates the world towards a goal. This is why the New Creation in the Bible is not simply a return to the Garden but has another key aspect added in – a city.

The image of a garden city is one that speaks of harmony between nature and technology. It is a goal that is yet to be realized, a goal that God has ordained, which ultimately God will accomplish, and a goal with God at its centre. It is vital to recapture this future 'promise' because, as Brian Brock comments, 'Technological practices, because experienced as delivering power and meaning, will tend to shimmer with the promise of satisfaction and salvation that only God can fulfill.'[6]

He is saying that too often technology tells a different story and puts before us the 'promise' of an alternative goal, one where humanity is the hero and God is written out (remember the transhumanists).

Recapturing God's story reframes life and technology within the wider narrative of creation and enables us to make right choices about technology, its possibilities and its limitations.

The bug in the system

A comedian called Louis C. K. jokes (in pretty fruity language) about how easily we get frustrated with technology, particularly when something like sending a text is being 'too slow': 'Give it a second, would ya?! Would you give it a second?! It's going to space – can you give it a second to get back from space? Is the speed of light too slow for you . . . is it?!' We can all identify with this frustration (and its silliness)! It hints at a deeper issue, a lack of gratitude for the gift of technology, a loss of wonder at what it can achieve. It hints that something has gone wrong. There is a bug in the system.

And it is not just our frequent frustration with technology. Think of how technology is used. The same innovations that can be powerfully life-enriching can also be highly destructive; social media can be used to raise millions of pounds for charity but it is also used to organize terrorism.

Remember too that technology is not neutral. It has its own ethic. Facebook may have the benefit of putting us in contact with more of our friends more regularly, but it has also reframed what we mean by the word 'friend' and ironically stripped it of a lot of its value and importance.

Twitter may have brought instant involvement in public debate for millions of people, but it has also reduced much of the public conversation to pithy hashtags. For all the good that technology undoubtedly does, we know there is a bug in the system.

Part of the reason we have been talking about the 'story' of technology is because we want to flag up that modern technology is not just about what it does but the way that it allows us to narrate life. This is the 'framing' dynamic we referred to in chapter 1. In the beginning God starts the great story that we are all part of, but very quickly someone comes in with a different narrative, a different way of framing things:

> Now the serpent was more crafty than any other beast of
> the field that the LORD God had made. He said to the woman,
> 'Did God actually say, "You shall not eat of any tree in the
> garden"? . . . You will not surely die. For God knows that when

you eat of it your eyes will be opened, and you will be like God, knowing good and evil.'
(Genesis 3:1-5)

The serpent's story is so compelling! He talks about freedom in the face of restriction and possibility in the face of limitation. He talks of being 'like God'. How this story has persisted and now is retold over and over again through modern technology! As Brian Brock comments:

> Technology is the pride of our age. Technology is sin when it becomes a way of life expressing a quest for power and self-aggrandisement. It is sin as life formed by the fetters of self-interest, without wonder at the goodness of existing creation, without concern for the neighbor. Here desire reigns, greedily making an empire of our wills.[7]

We can trace this narrative in three particular areas that concern modern technology: the human self, time, and the world we inhabit.[8]

The self

As we have said, modern technology tells a story and it is a story about humanity, but the story is twisted because it has become a story with the self – not God – at its centre.

Of course, to focus on people isn't necessarily a bad thing. Good design and functionality and service really are good. If people are at the heart of God's design then the best technology will be the technology that best enables human beings to flourish. The problem comes when God is painted out of the picture. We didn't create ourselves. To be a person is to be made by God. Without him, people become 'users' or 'consumers' and the consumer becomes king. This is topsy-turvy thinking at its utmost because the reality is that God is the only one under whose rule life can flourish. Whereas human beings are inclined to grasp hold of power for our own good, God uses his power to serve others in love.

Our distorted narrative is that we want to be king and we want everyone to serve us! As a result, too much of modern technology is geared the wrong way, promoting 'autonomy' (literally being a 'law to your self') over historic sources of authority, and exalting self over the service of others.

Time

You are in a department store and you hear the child whine, 'But Mummy, I want it now!' You roll your eyes as you mind-lessly wonder how long you are going to have to wait for your next phone upgrade! Impatience is one of the vices of our time.

The story of modern technology is a story of exponential growth and speed but, again, this is just a story. It is very difficult to measure accurately such 'growth'. Are we really inventing things faster? Even if we are, is the rate of growth getting ever quicker? Certainly we get things to market faster and there are more products out there, but how could we accurately measure the rate of change in innovation?

The serpent's lie promises instant satisfaction: 'When you eat of it your eyes will be opened.' God wanted Adam and Eve to wait, to hope in him and obey his instruction, trusting him enough to work towards the fulfilment of his promised future in his good time. He did not give them everything 'now'. As we have seen, he had finished his work of creation, but the finished creation was only the beginning. God's plan to fill creation with his glory under his royal, image-bearing children still remained to be fulfilled. They needed to be patient and allow the story to unfold. Instead they gave in to the sin of pride that places humankind over God. They refused the terms

As humans, we want instant satisfaction and not patiently wait for God's timing of God's gift. They thought they could manufacture a better future for themselves without God. They wanted the life he promised and they wanted it now. And so began the human story of immediacy. It continues today – patience is a commodity in short supply and the instant-fulfilment promise of digital technology seems to be making matters worse.

The world

It is amazing when you play with a young child how much joy he or she gets from simple things. When you release a balloon and it floats up to the ceiling the child giggles with delight: 'Again!' You do it again. The same reaction. No loss of joy, no boredom. 'Again!' You will get bored long before the toddler will! Why is it that a balloon can delight a child for hours day after day, but a brand-new computer can seem passé for an adult within moments of unboxing it?

Could it be linked back to a loss of a sense of gratitude for the gift of creation? Could it be that part of what keeps our wonder and joy alive is when we see the world not as formless 'stuff' that's just 'there' but as a gift from a loving God? In this regard the lie the serpent tells in the Garden has two dimensions to it. First, that God is holding something back from the man and woman, that there is something better he hasn't given – the knowledge of good and evil. Second, that this knowledge of good and evil is theirs to take, instead of seeing that God is the gift-giver who wisely holds some things back.

So today there is a sense of possession around modern technology. We think and talk all too easily of 'must have' gadgets. Questions of affordability and necessity are casualties in our desire to have more. As with self-centred autonomy and the demand for immediacy, our sense of entitlement and possession, instead of gratitude and wonder, is part of the bug in the system.

Rebooting the system

Bill Gates has admitted that having to press Control-Alt-Delete to reboot a Microsoft system was a mistake: 'We could have had a single button, but the guy who did the IBM keyboard design didn't wanna give us our single button.'[9] It seems ironic that such a famous button combination that has saved many a user from a system error was itself a mistake! One of the wonderful realizations is that in God's story his redemption (his 'reboot', to use the all-too-easy metaphor) was not a mistake. It was not plan B. The goal of creation has been forever the same.

This is important because, as we have already commented, God is not taking us back to the Garden and wiping out all the wonder of human design. This is often forgotten in popular depictions of heaven as a garden. (One friend we know described his (mis)understanding of God's promised future as 'a nudist colony in a rain forest'. He followed up with the logical question: 'Why would I want to spend eternity there?')

Under such a back-to-the-garden understanding, technology is a necessary evil after the Fall because work has been frustrated by the curse of Genesis 3. One imagines therefore that in the New Creation with the curse removed (and therefore no need for technology), we will all be subduing the earth by digging merrily with our bare hands!

William Blake really did technology no favours by the line in his poem (later a hymn) about 'those dark satanic mills'.[10] It wasn't technology of its own accord that brought darkness to England's green and pleasant land. The dark power of technology is the power for destruction in the hands of destructive people. Removing technology can't cure our problems, because technology didn't cause them.

We need to recapture a narrative of the Garden City as the goal to which creation is heading. This reframes technology and gives it new importance. We will still be innovating in eternity! Have you started to think about what technology will be like when it is cleansed from all human pride and selfishness, when it operates in perfect harmony with God and his creation? What innovations will we enjoy when there have been 10,000 years of unfettered, flawless, redeemed innovation, all to the glory of God and the flourishing of his world? Such a vision breathes new life into our technological endeavours. It also provides much-needed restraint as it brings modern technology under the umbrella of God's story.

The key question then is, what was God's Control-Alt-Delete? Whenever a system is rebooted there is a danger that all its original settings and work will be lost. You have to back it up first. What we want is a new system that works perfectly, so the bug is fixed, but that has not lost all the things that are precious and important to us.

How does God do this? As we have already noted, God's story is a story of humanity. So his redemption came through the perfect man Jesus Christ, who lived the perfect life none of us have lived, and died the death we deserve to die for trying to write God out of the story. As the prophet Isaiah put it, 'Upon him was the chastisement that brought us peace' (Isaiah 53:5). The resurrection life of Jesus then set in motion the great reboot of the world.

The New Creation will come about because it has started in Christ's resurrection body but, importantly, the New Creation does not completely wipe the system. It only cleanses the system of what is flawed, but it retains all the original settings and develops them towards the goal for which they were always intended. This is similarly what it means for human beings to become 'new creations' (see 2 Corinthians 5:17). We are not completely wiped of all that makes us unique and special, nor is every experience in this life cast away. We are rebooted in a way that keeps our initial integrity but purifies us of our flaws.

Oliver O'Donovan puts it well: 'The eschatological [future] transformation of the world is neither the mere repetition of the created world nor its negation. It is its fulfilment, its telos or end.'[11]

All this has three particular implications for us to draw out.

1. The perfect life

Jesus Christ is both perfect God and perfect man. He shows us what life lived fully engaged in the world in worship of God the Father looks like. He might not have lived in the modern technological age, but he engaged with the technology of his own day. He was a carpenter, he fished, he made fires, he prepared meals, he sailed on boats across the Sea of Galilee and he loved the city – weeping over Jerusalem. It is easy for us to forget that he lived and flourished in a technologized society (albeit one from 2,000 years ago). He did not eschew technology and live in the desert. The key virtues we will pick up throughout the book – thankfulness, patience, humility, service, faith – are seen uniquely in him and must be vital in shaping how we live in our time.

2. Life now

While we wait for the full effects of Jesus' redemption to be realized, we don't wait passively. We are to work towards that realization now. God sends us his Spirit so that the reboot, though partial this side of the New Creation, is nonetheless substantial. The Spirit works in us to reorientate our lives within God's story. This reorientation is aimed at life in the new world that God is making. We enter into this world by faith and begin to enjoy it even now, as we seek to engage positively with technology in the service of God, people and the world.

This reorientation also means a thorough revision of any ways in which we may have bought into the story of 'the world against God' or 'the world without God'. Technology taken as a right we are entitled to, not a gift to receive with gratitude. Technology used for our own ends at the expense of others. Technology perpetuating systemic injustice while we turn a blind eye. God's love should move us to repentance for our misuse of his good world. The destructive power of technology and its effects on human life and the created environment are there to be seen in our world. Technology seems to distance us from responsibility, but the distance is an illusion.

There is a relationship between the food we eat and the way it is farmed, the clothes we wear and the kind of factories they are produced in, the attention parents fail to pay and the absence children feel, the ways we travel and the fuel we use, the messages we send and the lives of the people who receive them. We will need to reflect and repent of the ways we have lived against the grain of creation. This repentance will mean an ongoing and active reorientation by faith in better ways of life.

3. Life now empowered by the Spirit

Whether or not you are a Christian, the message of repentance can easily seem oppressive. Does God really call on people to reorientate their lives in such a thoroughgoing way? The answer, of course, is yes. He wouldn't be loving if he demanded anything less. But that's not all there is to say.

He wouldn't be God if he called on us to change on our own. The deepest work of God's Spirit is to unite us to Jesus Christ. Christian faith is always a trust in his work for us.

Christian repentance is always a reorientation of life in view of what he has already done. Looking to Christ, we see the true effects of our attempts to write God out of the story. Jesus – the infinitely selfless man – is laid low on the cross for our technological pride and self-centredness. Jesus – the wonderfully patient man – experiences the full extent of God's anger at our impatience and desire for immediacy. Jesus – the perfectly thankful man – pays on the cross for our ingratitude despite the many gifts God lavishes on us.

This forgiveness is God's great gift to be received by faith. As we increasingly know the significance of what Jesus achieved through his life, death and resurrection, the Spirit will work in us to remake us into the people we were made to be. As the words of the hymn put it:

Holy Spirit, living Breath of God,
Breathe new life into my willing soul.
Bring the presence of the risen Lord
To renew my heart and make me whole.
Cause Your Word to come alive in me;
Give me faith for what I cannot see;
Give me passion for Your purity.
Holy Spirit, breathe new life in me.[12]

To live in this modern technological age requires that we grasp the great story we are all in – not only its beginning, nor just the bug in the system, but also the reboot that God has begun. The next chapter unpacks how this story 'interfaces' with our technological lives at each important level of engagement.

Questions

1. Intuitively how do you feel about technology: suspicious, excited, concerned, confused, hopeful? Why not ask your friends how they feel about it and reflect on what it is that shapes different responses?
2. How does knowing that technology is part of God's creation and part of what it means to 'be fruitful and subdue the earth' challenge your answer to question 1?
3. In what ways do you find yourself buying into the story of progress?
4. Which of the vices in the 'bug in the system' section are most obvious in your life (self-centredness and autonomy, impatience and immediacy, entitlement and possession)? Why not spend some time confessing them to God and then speak to a friend who could help you work at this area?
5. How does seeing the New Creation as both a garden and a city challenge popular ideas about heaven? What is there about this that excites you and makes you long to be there?

The interface

So far we have spent most of our time dealing with the theory and theology of technology. When, you might be asking, will we get to what this all means in practice? It's a valid question, but one that can lead us into difficulty if the pursuit of practice has a habit of bypassing our brain.

The aim of this chapter is to get practical in a way that joins theory and practice together. We want to help you to get into the practice of thinking through how the gospel of Jesus Christ will always be both a 'yes' and a 'no' to technology. This gospel reflection on technology will lead to changed behaviours, but we believe those behaviours will only have a long-term impact if they are underpinned by careful and correct thinking.

Technology seems to offer near-instant solutions to our problems and so it lures us into a quick-fix mindset. After the first seminar Ed gave on technology, a woman came up and said, 'I'm sorry I couldn't come to your seminar but I would like to know whether or not my daughter should be using Facebook.' Where to start? Her motives may have been good but she needed to ask some better questions. Could it be that the desire for an instant yes/no answer is as much a symptom of our digital age as too many hours spent on Facebook?

Of course we are not saying that everyone needs to read ten books for each question they have. But perhaps one of the key practices we might need to cultivate is that of reflection instead of knee-jerk responses. Fools rush in. You will know this if you have ever texted, emailed or tweeted in anger. Minutes later you realize the error of your ways and frantically try to find a way to recall or erase your mistake.

First, reflection requires engagement. We began by considering questions about the nature of technology and the goal of life because we think they are really important. If we don't engage technology at a deep level, then any new practices we adopt will have as much energy as the battery on a five-year-old laptop.

Second, engagement is not just to be done alone. Thinking and talking together with others is important, and there is nowhere better for this conversation than in the intergenerational community of the church. It is a community that should be committed to integrating what it is learning into the daily practices of life. Perhaps you could start a conversation at church about some area of technology that you use – texting and its effect on relationships, or Twitter and its effect on debate? Who knows, you may learn a lot through it and you may help others as well.

Third, engagement requires time. Isn't patience one of the virtues that Christ embodied and that his Spirit is forming within his people? As we will see in chapter 6, the modern world is far from patient; it rushes to find a solution, often leaving the main issue on the shelf. Adopting the counter-practice of intentionally reflecting, along with others, on the nature of life in the digital age is itself productively countercultural.

So here's our first lesson about practice: good practice is always reflective. When we are faced with questions like: 'How much time should we spend on social media?', 'Should smartphones be banned in schools?' and 'Should the Internet be regulated?', we should resist the urge to 'solve' our perceived problem with superficial answers. After all, life was made to be lived, not to be solved. This is the reason we have added some questions at the end of each chapter (and haven't given the answers at the back of the book!).

We don't think these are all the questions that could be asked. They might not necessarily be the best ones – you may want to add more of your own. Our aim is to catalyse a conversation that serves to move more and more people from being 'users' of technology to 'reflective practitioners', joining together with others to embrace practices of technology that are truly ways of life.

'Yes' and 'no'

For the activists reading this, be assured that reflection is deeply practical. All our thinking takes place within a life of engaging with technology that is already underway. We can't press 'pause' on the world in order to work out how to live well before we 're-enter'. All our thoughts and actions about technology must be worked out in real time and in real life.

This book is no exception. It is 7pm on a December evening and we are working together in the heart of London, in a flat overlooking London's Old Street. Fifty metres away is 'tech roundabout', the centre of London's up-and-coming digital technology district. The UK headquarters of Google are just around the corner.

As you might have guessed, we aren't writing this book out on parchment, dipping our quills in ink. We are working on laptops with some brilliant word-processing software called Scrivener. We don't know where you are when you are reading this (although there are ways of finding out!), but you will be well aware of how technology is a part of your life. Our different contexts are important. They are the times and places about which we must reflect. They are the times and places in (or from) which we must act out our obedience to Christ.

How does the gospel meet and shape the lives we are already living? We are persuaded that following Christ doesn't simply mean pressing the 'off' switch (if you can find it, which these days isn't as easy as it might sound). Of course, there are times when active disconnection will be a good practice to adopt, but we need to learn how to follow Christ online also. The pattern of life we want to advocate here is the pattern of the gospel, which confronts the world with both God's 'yes' and his 'no'.

God's 'yes'

Just as we must reflect from within the story of technology, so the wonder of the gospel is that God doesn't only control history from without but also steps into history in Jesus Christ. He entered into the story to change it. He submitted himself to the limits of the world, this world, working from within real life and space and time.

The details of the Christmas story about Mary and Joseph and the Roman census and the trip to Bethlehem are not just there to keep the children interested. These details are essential to the gospel. God came into this world as a man in order to remake humanity, in order to bring life even to this digital world.

In living as a man, Christ affirmed the goodness of the world God made and showed God's love for it. When we get a new gadget, the old one is laid to rest in the technology graveyard (there is one in every home: in Ed's house it's a box in the loft full of old Nokia mobiles, on which many happy hours were spent playing *Snake*).

We lose interest so quickly in things that are old and don't work like they used to, but God has never lost interest in his broken world. Christ suffered for it and rose again to save it – you don't get much more of a 'yes' than that. In rising from the dead, and standing physically on the soil of this earth, Christ showed his defeat of death and loudly declared that God's plan to bring his creation to the glorious end of his story will surely be fulfilled. As we remember at Christmas, 'The light shines in the darkness, and the darkness has not overcome it' (John 1:5).

As we've mentioned previously, one vital application of this is giving thanks. Giving thanks has a powerful way of re-awakening our hearts to the wonder of everyday things we too easily take for granted.

Another practice linked to giving thanks is praise. Praise is a very basic human response. We praise the latest technology when we tell our friends about its great features. Online reviews praise the innovations of a new product. It is so natural that we rarely reflect on what we are doing. In and of itself this is not wrong. But it becomes wrong if the praise of the object usurps the praise of its Giver. Perhaps one of the key ways we can combat the idolatry embedded in the materialism of our digital world is through cultivating a heart of praise to God for technology rather than just a praise of technology.

God's 'no'

God's 'yes' gives us a positive message to proclaim to the world. The gospel really is good news. But for the good news to be truly good, the 'yes' must also come with a 'no'. We know this is true from the time we spend on Facebook, where we are only allowed to 'like'. This is intentional: Facebook wants to cultivate positive social interactions and fears that negative sentiment will turn people away (imagine the fights that would break out online if people were able to say with a click how much they didn't like each other).

But Facebook users aren't satisfied. There are things we dislike – sometimes rightly, sometimes not – and we want to be able to express them. When it is so easy to 'like' and impossible to 'dislike' we are well aware that the 493 'likes' next to the photo of the three-year-old with spaghetti in her hair are not incredibly meaningful. The point is more serious than it sounds. In order for the light to win, the darkness of the world cannot be avoided: it must be defeated. At the cross, that's exactly what Jesus did.

Throughout the Bible, darkness speaks of the absence of God, the absence of his creative activity and the absence of his presence as he turns his face away in judgment on human sin. As Christ hung on the cross, the Gospel writers tell us that 'when the sixth hour had come, there was darkness over the land until the ninth hour' (Mark 15:33). This was no eclipse. For three hours, in the middle of the day (the sixth hour is midday), the world that had condemned God's Son to death found itself shrouded under the darkness of God's judgment.

For the light to win, the darkness of the world cannot be avoided: it must be defeated.

This picture of judgment is consistent with God's response to human wickedness throughout history. When God turns his face away from evil, he isn't turning a blind eye. He isn't a passive observer, powerless to do anything about a world broken by sin. The darkness is God's judgment – his clear word of 'no' – his declaration that sin will not go on forever, leaving the powerful as history's victors and the poor forgotten in the past.

Jesus shows us this so clearly in his life – he condemned sin wherever it was found and spoke of its ultimate source, not in social structures, but in the human heart (Mark 7). That same 'no' is still God's word today against the sins that characterize the digital age. The virtual world is not beyond his attention. He still hates corruption, oppression, self-righteousness, pride, lust, anger and greed.

You don't have to look hard to see how these sins have technological manifestations that hang darkly over the online presence of goodness and beauty and generosity and justice and friendship and collaboration and truth.

This 'no' of the gospel will need to work out in our lives. Restraint and abstinence are not virtues promoted by our digital age, but they are arguably more vital today than ever before. The old Burger King advert said, 'You want it your way – you got it!' Digital information technologies often provide the platforms that fuel consumerism through 'personalized browser experiences' and 'preference settings'. In the UK, marketing agencies know that the biggest users of technology are often the lowest income groups. People get into high levels of debt on credit cards because products have become 'must haves', regardless of financial means.

Fasting from food reminds us that human beings cannot live on bread alone but on every word that comes from the mouth of the Lord (Deuteronomy 8:3). Why not try fasting from technology for a time? When was the last time you turned your phone off? Not just on silent (where it still vibrates in your pocket and distracts you) but actually turned it off? I (Pete) have the habit of going on a prayer retreat once or twice a year. When I go, I turn my phone off. In a quiet moment, my hand reaches for the phone to check BBC Sport or Facebook, but the phone's not there. What happens next is striking. I start to notice my thoughts. Perhaps a Bible verse is called to mind. Maybe I notice my surroundings more acutely.

Or why not keep a journal for a week of your Facebook habits or some other platform that you spend a lot of time on? Do you know how much you use it and when you use it? Chances are it is more than you think.

Perhaps reflect on what your usage tells you. Are you using it as a means of escapism? Is it where you go to when you feel anxious? Is it the first thing you look at in the morning and the last thing at night (interestingly a place Deuteronomy 6:7 encourages us to keep for God's Word in Scripture)? If so, is that a good thing or could it be harmful? What might saying an appropriate 'no' to it look like?

Holding 'yes' and 'no' together

Given God's consistent 'no' to sin, the incredible thing, as we return to Christ hanging on the cross and the land covered in darkness, is what Jesus says: 'My God, my God, why have you forsaken me?' (Mark 15:34). The wonder of the gospel, and the reason the cross of Christ is at its heart, is that at the cross, God's 'no' of judgment was taken by Jesus Christ. Darkness covered the land, and yet he was the one forsaken.

The resurrection 'yes' then brings with it an amazing promise: for all who come to Jesus, God's 'no' of condemnation has been spoken already to Christ.

The world without Christ has no way of overcoming the darkness. The best the world can do is to try to limit its consequences through public policy or education or personal development. These are good things, and can make a difference, but they can't deal with the problem at its core because they can't change the inclination of our hearts. Without this deep resolution, the world is ultimately left trying to avoid the darkness or pretending it doesn't matter as much as we sometimes think.

But we know it matters; we see and we feel its effects in the world. In Christ's death and resurrection, God's 'no' and 'yes' hold together. Sin is condemned – defeated, not avoided – and there is new life for this world that God loves.

Lesslie Newbigin was a missionary in India in the twentieth century. He returned home to Britain in 1974 with some deep insights about how the gospel could meet the increasingly secular culture that he found. The gospel will never impact the culture, he said, when either God's 'yes' or his 'no' are suppressed. If we cannot say 'yes' to culture then we are not recognizing God's common grace and will be dismissed as culturally irrelevant 'nay-sayers'. But if we cannot say 'no' to culture, then we have no ability to challenge and change its embedded flaws. Both are needed and at the same time.

So it is with technology. Failing to recognize the gospel's 'no' will lead us to an uncritical adoption of many of the flawed technological patterns and practices. We need to guard against a naivety that cannot see beyond technology's sheen to the embedded injustices and destructive behaviour patterns it masks.

On the other hand, there is also a danger if we fail to apply the 'yes'. We will end up rejecting the wrong thing – technology instead of sin – and the result will be a church that is irrelevant to the digital world.

What is more, since we cannot escape the world entirely, even the most hardened techno-sceptic will end up taking on many more of the practices of the digital world than he or she will ever give credit for.

The 'yes' and 'no' of the gospel operate at the level of both reflection and practice. These two aspects allow us to make important distinctions in our understanding of technology. No technology is absolutely good or bad. There will always be elements of both.

Consider, for example, the way we take photographs, now that our smartphone comes with a high-quality built-in camera and allows us to modify our photos with Instagram before we share them with others. Surely we can see much good in this. We can take photos that capture the beauty of the world or of a moment with friends or family. We can share photos around the world in an instant and so share in the experiences of others. Ed's brother has just sent through a stunning photo of the Inca settlement at Machu Picchu in the mountains of Peru.

But, at the same time, the 'no' of the gospel speaks to the ways in which smartphone photography can hinder an appreciation of God's world. Sometimes we are so busy 'capturing the moment' on our phones that the moment actually passes us by. Sometimes we are so caught up in applying the right Instagram filter to the photo of a sunset that we miss the changing hues of dusk right in front of our eyes.

If you enjoy thinking about the culture we live in, then hopefully this 'yes' and 'no' approach will fuel your reflection. But there is an important objection to consider here. If you are more practically minded it might well be yours: aren't there occasions when we don't need to reflect but just need to act? Aren't there occasions when following Christ should lead us to simply say 'no'?

These questions often come from a passionate desire to maintain integrity and avoid compromise. And so far as they do, they reveal an impulse which we affirm. There are websites we should not visit, apps we should not use, emails we should not send, games we should not let our children play. You can add to the list.

But remember, we aren't advocating reflection in opposition to practice, but together with it. Practice is inevitable since we are always living according to some pattern of behaviour or another, and there are times when the best practice to adopt will be one of rejection. However, even in these cases, the fact that we should say a firm 'no' should not stop reflection but fuel it. If we dismiss something without ongoing thought, we leave ourselves open to the underlying issue which has been avoided but not addressed. This then frequently resurfaces in another area that goes unnoticed. Concerned parents, for example, might impose a blanket ban on their children accessing the Internet in their bedroom. That might well be a wise restriction. But if the engagement ends there, how will their children be equipped to deal with what they see on their friend's smartphone in the playground at school?

Where there seems to be a clear clash between technology and God's Word, it is a good way forward to act in line with our conscience and then follow up the decision with reflection. The decision alone is not sufficient because there are still questions to consider: what are we saying 'no' to, and why? And what is the nature of the 'no'? Is it 'no, we should never use this app' or 'no, using that online retailer is against my conscience' or 'no, "liking" that photo would support a cause that is opposed to the gospel' or 'no, you are too young for that game'? And is the 'no' in one case related to practices in other areas that might also need to change? Every urgent action calls for further patient reflection.

As an example, the question of technology, food and farming is one I (Ed) have been working through at home with my wife recently. Following a conversation with some friends we felt it was clear that we should stop buying battery-farmed chickens. The logic was clear to us:

- In buying food we bear a level of responsibility for the way the food is produced.
- Battery farming is not in accord with God's command to steward creation with care.
- We should no longer buy battery chickens.

So we stopped: a clear 'no'. But that was just the start of a journey that has left us trying to reflect on what and how we eat (we haven't yet addressed table manners!).

Of course we haven't solved all the issues. Should we only buy food when we can be sure how it has been farmed? What level of care for animals is required in the farming and how do we balance this if our family is trying to watch its budget? The questions go on and on. The point is not that we have sorted everything out, but rather by engaging we are realizing more of the implications of our consumption and in some small way becoming better stewards of God's creation.

Hopefully this chapter has given a sense of how we can approach life in the digital world. We need to grow as 'reflective practitioners', being willing to ask questions about life in the digital world but always recognizing that we are asking those questions as people who are already shaped by the culture we live in and the technology it has led us to adopt.

The practices that have become accepted patterns of life will shape our questions, just as the answers to the questions should shape our practices. In all this, we need to keep remembering that reflective practice is ongoing. New technologies will continue to raise new questions and bring new challenges.

That is why these three chapters have been focused more on 'how to reflect on technological practice' than just jumping in with solutions. We believe that the 'how to' element will be of longer-term benefit than any solutions we may propose, and we fully expect that as you reflect on your own practice you will come up with answers that will probably be better than ours!

Not that we are going to stop here. In the chapters ahead we will consider some key aspects of life in the digital world and some particular technologies. We will offer our own analysis and understanding of how the gospel's 'yes' and 'no' might work, drawing out some key themes. As we do, our aim is not to close down the conversation about technology but to play a helpful part in opening it up.

Questions

1. What is the problem with separating theory from practice?
2. How might you join with others in intentionally reflecting on your practices of life when it comes to technology?
3. Do you see technology as one of God's blessings? Why, or why not? As suggested in the chapter, spend some time giving thanks for the technology.
4. What would be the technological device, platform or app that you think would be hardest for you to 'fast' from? Why? Why not try doing without it for a day and reflect on what you learn?
5. Why must our engagement with technology always include both 'yes' and 'no'? Which is your natural inclination, saying 'yes' or giving a strong 'no'? Practise cultivating the other attitude as well.

6. Think of some different technologies you use (e.g. email, WhatsApp, BBC iPlayer, Kindle). What practices of life have these technologies brought with them? Start drawing out some aspects of the gospel's 'yes' and 'no'.

Part 2

I tweet therefore I am

What should I write on my Twitter profile? Surely it isn't that complicated? Simply enter a few choice words into the box that will give people a sense of who I am.

But if it is so easy, why can't I decide what to say?

I know the kind of impression I want to give: thoughtful but not intense, funny without trying too hard, like those I admire but also unique. What can I write that will be authentically me?

And then there's the question of the photo. Serious, quirky, smart, relaxed, with kids, on holiday, snapshot, posed? There are far too many to choose from. I spend ages scrolling through the options, but none of them are really the thing I am looking for.

Why am I wasting so much time on this? If I just thought sensibly about it for a moment, I would soon come to terms with the fact it is not the real 'me' anyway. It's just a profile.

The challenge Twitter has presented me with isn't simply to write a few things about myself. The challenge is to decide who exactly I am in this brave new socially networked world.

The dilemma is not unique to Twitter. It's actually a foundational question we all face. The Danish thinker Søren Kierkegaard went so far as to say our fundamental problem is that we build our identity on anything but God. As with many questions the digital world raises, the question is not new. It is as old as humanity. But it is pressed on us in a particular way in a virtual environment where attaching images, ideas, experiences and preferences to our personal icon effectively defines who we are. If that is the only 'me' that others see, is that the only 'me' there is? We don't believe that it is, but the question is powerful enough to make many people anxiously monitor their online image.

Don't get us wrong. It's not that we all go online with the intention of portraying ourselves to the world in a certain way. We don't all scroll for hours through photos in order to impress others or pore over every word of each instant message so that we come across exactly right. That's not how things are most of the time. Most of the time we just go for it – posting, messaging, tweeting, uploading – without giving it a second thought. But those messages and images are still defining who we are online even when we don't mean them to. That's why we are so concerned to know what people are saying in response to our witty comment or to see how many people liked our latest celebrity selfie.

What kind of person have you been online in the last few months?

Have you ever reviewed your timeline? Or gone back and looked at your Twitter feed or browser history? Why not have a look?

What do you learn about yourself? What kind of person have you been online in the last few months? What has mattered most to you? Where have you spent your time? Do you recognize the person you are seeing? Is that person happy?

A recent study into the effects of Facebook by researchers at the University of Michigan found that heavy use of the social network was linked to increased dissatisfaction. 'Facebook is bad for you' was the grabbing headline as it appeared in the media.[1] Constant use of social media is making people miserable. Perhaps that has been your experience, or at least one aspect of it. What the study suggested was that constant awareness of the positive images and experiences of others made people more and more anxious about their own lives. Either we play the game (which is a bit like Top Trumps) and post a highlight of our own, or we resign ourselves to what seems like a fact: our life is just not as satisfying as the lives of our friends. And that is a thought that takes root over time, growing a sense of insignificance and unhappiness.

Maybe you have felt something of this dynamic at work. A video you posted has gone viral and you have basked in the reflected glory of your newsfeed lighting up. But then the next post appears, and the next, and the next, and you keep checking your phone but there is almost nothing by way of likes or comments. You feel gloom, not glory. You see a post from an old friend: 'What a week. Promotion at work, Jonny took first steps, just exchanged on our new house #blessed'. You click 'like' and genuinely do share the excitement. But you are still left empty, because the exciting life isn't yours.

This chapter seeks to explore the roots of this love/hate relationship we have with our online profile. Our aim is to go beyond the media critique of Facebook that raises the problem but offers few resources for a positive way forward. We will seek to dig deeper into the identity question that underlies the power of the network to influence our happiness. We will explore how this question is grounded in the story of life that gave birth to the anxiety of the modern world. And we will consider the difference it makes to actively connect our online life with an appreciation of who we are as defined by the God who made us. With him there is life beyond the swing between glory and gloomy that seems to be a feature of so many people's online experience.

I tweet therefore I am

As we have said, these 'big questions' concerning who we are and what it means to live well are not new. A key time when they were being radically rethought and reimagined was during what history has called the Enlightenment. Scientific advance, the rise of the printing press, and a century of religious conflict in Europe during the 1500s had called into question the place of God and the accepted order of society. Change was in the air.

One of the key thinkers of the time was René Descartes, who wrote his famous *Meditations* in 1639. In a world where the old certainties of life had been challenged, Descartes was left looking for solid ground on which to build his philosophy. It is difficult today to get a sense of how radical his approach was. He started by stripping everything away, all the conventional sources of answers to life's big questions – traditions of thought, religious authorities, social institutions; they were all put to one side. None of them could provide the certainty he was seeking. Eventually he was left with one thing on which he could surely build: 'I think, therefore I am.' On the sentiment of this famous statement the modern world was established. A world built on the certainty of our own understanding.

You may be relieved to know that we are not going to try to critique René, though we think that, brilliant as he was, his project was flawed from the beginning. The reason we refer to him is that his project to find certainty based on self-definition in an age of change and turmoil is still with us nearly 400 years on.

We live in a culture that is sceptical of authority. The oppression inflicted by those in power is written through the history of the twentieth century – a century we are understandably keen to put behind us. Eager to move forward, we have followed Descartes ever more radically, seizing the opportunity to define who we are as the fundamental human right. It is in this context that the virtual world presents us with a seductive promise: you can shape your own identity. You are free to cast off all that you dislike and be the person who is creative and intelligent and thoughtful and funny and kind.

In this world you are free from the constraints of your past and commitments of the present. You must decide for yourself who you are and what path you will follow. Let nothing get in the way. You are free to direct your own journey through life. You can avoid all those places that you would rather not travel to: places called failure and frustration and loneliness and loss and grief and guilt and disappointment and death.

Instead you can choose to head only to those places that will affirm and encourage you: places flowing with milk and honey, places where you can linger long into the night because the gates are always open and the sun never sets. And imagine hundreds of friends supporting you in your quest and hundreds of followers eager to go along with you. It is a pretty compelling proposition, isn't it? No wonder so many people are drawn to the online world.

The virtual world's promise is presented to us with a set of online tools and technologies to make it happen. If you don't want to be alone, then you can find a forum where your opinion is valued and where friends will 'like' your post.

If you want to be right, then the chances are there is a blog out there that shares your opinion.

If you don't like how you look, then 'Instagram' your image (or there's Photoshop for a more thorough make-over!).

It seems we haven't moved far. 'I tweet therefore I am' #Renérevisited

What's in a name?

There is much that is attractive about this vision of life. We don't have to deny it. In fact, Christians should be the last ones to deny the goodness of the world. The most positive aspects actually depend on the gospel of Jesus Christ. There is much for us to say 'yes' to.

In traditional societies, identity comes from collective institutions, like the ones René was kicking against. Think of surnames: many of them came about because a person was defined by their family, their trade and their social position. 'Jackson' communicated that someone was the son of Jack. Depending on who Jack was, that could be good or bad. 'Smith' tells us that this person's forefather worked as a smith – a tradesman. 'Masterton' conveys that this person was 'master of the town' – clearly someone important.

Such sources of identity may have been quite stable, but you can see the problem straight away: they are very constraining. What if everyone in your community loathed your namesake Jack? The die is cast even before you have the chance to express who you are.

Perhaps you have experienced that kind of typecasting? You have been put in a box before you even had a chance to present yourself? Perhaps because of the school you went to, or the way you speak, or the job you do, or the part of town you live in, or because of your gender, race or age. How did you feel? How did you respond?

Social media allows us to be ourselves in a way that is remarkably free from such constraints. In very conservative societies, this freedom can allow life to flourish. Think of Malala Yousafzai who comes from the Swat valley in Pakistan, a region controlled by the Taliban. As a young girl in that community all the power dynamics were against her: gender, age, education. In that region girls had frequently been banned from attending school. Yet through writing an online blog for the BBC under a pseudonym she was given a voice to the wider world.

When the Taliban attempted to kill Malala in 2012, she survived and her story went viral. She is the youngest ever winner of the Nobel Peace Prize and in their 29 April 2013 issue, *Time* magazine named her one of 'The 100 most influential people in the world' for her work in campaigning for girls' rights to education.

For the way that social media allows us to be the persons we really are and express our freedom, we should be thankful. There is more fuel here for the practice of gratitude as a digital virtue that we thought about in the previous chapter.

What's to 'dislike'?

However, as much as we can affirm the personal freedoms promoted online, there are problems as well – things that the gospel says 'no' to. Are we really able to define ourselves online and find there the purpose and meaning that makes life flourish?

My difficulty in deciding what to write on my Twitter profile suggests that defining ourselves in the digital world, while attractive, is not quite as straightforward as we might think. Consider the twin mantras often posted on social media: 'Just be yourself' and 'Be who you want to be'. 'Just be yourself' implies there is a pre-defined 'me' that I need to be true to. 'Be who you want to be' suggests that my identity is yet to be determined. Both can't be right.

Equally, the technology that promises more freedom often seems to enslave us. Think for a moment about the way you engage with the digital world and the way you treat the gadgets that act as the gateway to life online.

Ever get the feeling that your iPhone / Android is calling the shots in your life? You know there won't be anything important to read but you have to check Facebook. You know it doesn't count for much but you have to check how many followers you've got. You sleep with your phone next to your bed, since it is also your alarm clock, but as it wakes you up it draws you in. You can't get out of bed before at least checking in with your social network. And then you really should check your Twitter feed, and Instagram, and . . .

When Facebook tells my friends that I am at home with my children, my children will tell you that I am actually on Facebook with my friends!

If you can't see this pattern in your own life, think about those around you. Do you ever get the sense that your friends and family are physically present but are really on another planet? People are yet to master the ability to be in two places at once, so the reality is that when Facebook tells my friends that I am at home with my children, my children will tell you that I am actually on Facebook with my friends!

It is easy for parents to be anxious about the way their children are engaging with technology. The anxiety is often well founded. Violent video games do impact the way children learn to relate to others. Online porn is harmful. Endless screen time does make it harder for our kids to concentrate. Of course, children can engage positively with tech too and parents can help them. But perhaps the first step is for parents to take more notice of the concerns of their children for the way the parents are using technology. It struck me (Ed) recently that the struggle to encourage my three-year-old to give up the iPad and play in the garden is strikingly similar to the struggle my three-year-old has when I am checking work emails on my phone and he wants to go to the park. Sound familiar to anyone else? Maybe it's just me?

The attraction of the digital world is that we are connected and in control. The reality is that the network is far from passive in the way our lives are changing. The attractional power of life online is entirely intentional. It is a direct out-working of the way the digital world has been engineered. Facebook, for instance, employs psychologists and social scientists along with computer programmers in order to understand how we behave online, and then increase the time we spend on their network.

We are urged to befriend the maximum number of people so that our newsfeed is constantly updating. The online space fuels positive feedback to draw us in. There is no 'dislike' button since negative emotion has been shown to send people running for cover. Even in 2015 when Facebook introduced a 'dislike' it was only to empathise with posts about sad events and not to bring in a genuine 'dislike' to temper the 'likes'. And, of course, it isn't only Facebook. The whole social media landscape is sculpted this way.

Finally there's the problem of disconnection. Just the other day Pete went to do a talk at a Student Christian Union and looked beforehand at the profile picture of who was meeting him. In reality the student was so different from his profile that Pete walked straight past him, twice! It made him wonder what else on his profile was different.

This hints at the problem of fragmentation. For all that we have the freedom to redefine ourselves, there is a sense that we all long for those rare virtues of simplicity and integrity. Dave Eggers' satire of Google, in his novel *The Circle*, may be deliberately overstated, but he captures well the attraction and challenge of online identity as he describes a new invention:

> TruYou – one account, one identity, one password, one payment system, per person. There were no more passwords, no multiple identities. Your devices knew who you were, and your one identity – the TruYou, unbendable and unmaskable – was the person paying, signing up, responding, viewing and reviewing, seeing and being seen.[2]

To practise integrity in terms of our online persona doesn't necessarily mean sharing every experience and photograph. In fact, it certainly doesn't. Please don't do that!

Integrity is not about letting it all hang out when we are online. Most people know well enough that there is a time and a place for different kinds of disclosure. Reviewing your Facebook feed from time to time and considering the kind of online presence you are cultivating is a wise move. Perhaps ask a few friends to give you some honest feedback about how your posts come across on their newsfeed. You might also ask them how they think your online and offline appearances match up. This is an important question since integrity is less about the extent of our disclosure and more about its consistency. It is important to make sure there is no a chasm between the online 'you' and the offline 'you'.

Finding a way forward – back to Geneva

Last night my laptop suggested a better way forward: 'You must restart for updates to take effect.' So let's hit 'refresh' on our browser and remember where we've come from.

In central Geneva is CERN (the European Organization for Nuclear Research) where in 1989 Sir Tim Berners-Lee invented the World Wide Web. The first ever website was hosted on a NeXT computer, and this original web server is still there.

Across the city from CERN, in the centre of Geneva, stands St Pierre's Cathedral, first built in the twelfth century on a site where there had already been a church for 400 years. In a fast-moving virtual world, the age and physical presence of this vast building is a reminder of the enduring strength of humankind's desire to worship, and the worldwide network that is formed by followers of Christ.

Five hundred years before Berners-Lee, St Peter's was the stage and Geneva the theatre at a significant point in another worldwide revolution. The development of the printing press had paved the way for ideas to spread like never before, and the biggest story of the day was that told by Geneva's most famous preacher and theologian, John Calvin (1509–64).

What Calvin did in the sixteenth century was to rediscover the deep truth of God's story for humanity and reconnect it to the lives of those in his generation. To understand rightly who we are, we need to listen afresh to that story.

Who are we? The question that we started with has been hanging over this chapter. It is about time we thought about an answer that we can build our lives on. Here Calvin can help us. In his famous *Institutes of the Christian Religion*, Calvin describes the world as the theatre of God's glory, with human beings as actors on God's stage.

We are *Homo adorans*, made to worship God by living under his liberating authority in the great drama of life. Worship is not an antiquated concept, irrelevant in this digital age. To worship something is to assign it ultimate importance in life, to let it define your identity. This is the key issue of our lives. There is no neutrality: fail to worship the true and living God and we will worship something else; we will worship anything else. Calvin famously said that our minds are idol-making factories.[3] An idol is anything we worship apart from God. To put it in more modern terms, he is saying that if we do not receive our identity from God as a gift, then we will constantly be searching for and inventing other sources of identity. Whatever that source of identity is effectively becomes our god, our idol.

To argue, like this, that the problem of modern identity is the ancient problem of idolatry sounds pretty extreme. Stick with us here. Idols are not only ancient statues but any aspect of God's creation that we take to be ultimate. Their power comes from the fact that idols are good aspects of God's world that we relate to as if they were God.

Our appearance is a good example. Physical beauty is a gift of God, a wonderful aspect of how he made us. But it is so easy to relate to the way we look as if it is our own possession. Rather than receiving the way we look as a gift and responding with gratitude to God, if we own our self-image then we have only ourselves to thank for how we look. And we have only ourselves to blame when we can't stand what we see.

The pressure this creates can be intense. We cultivate and select each photo we post. We are always rating ourselves and wanting others to affirm our own rating with theirs. We may not say it out loud, but 'How do I look?' is the hidden comment under each photo. 'You look incredible' is the glory-inducing comment that we delight in.

The problem is, looks fail us. We know that the image online is only one perspective. It's not the whole picture. And as we grow older the whole picture doesn't seem to improve. In the Instagram age, where every phone is a camera and every experience a photo opportunity, almost everyone is concerned with how they look. Even the people who carefully cultivate the opposite impression often care more than they let on.

Building our identity on our looks ultimately can only fail us. The same is true of identities built on our abilities, careers, intelligence, recognition, family, friends. All of these things are good things, which makes them the most likely candidates to take the place that only God can rightly hold.

Perhaps now we can see why social media is so alluring. Robbed of a secure identity rooted in God's love, social media promises so many different identities: popular, witty, intelligent, beautiful, busy, important, connected . . . the list goes on. The problem is that while all of these are good things, they are not good enough or secure enough to be assigned ultimate importance in our lives.

The writer David Foster Wallace died in 2008. In 2005 he addressed a cohort of graduating students about life and their identity:

> . . . here's something else that's true. In the day-to-day trenches of adult life, there is no such thing as atheism. There is no such thing as not worshipping. Everybody worships. The only choice we get is what to worship. And an outstanding reason for choosing some sort of god or spiritual-type thing to worship – be it JC or Allah, be it Yahweh or the Wiccan mother-goddess or the Four Noble Truths or some infrangible set of ethical principles – is that pretty much anything else you worship will eat you alive. If you worship money and things –

if they are where you tap real meaning in life – then you will never have enough. Never feel you have enough. It's the truth. Worship your own body and beauty and sexual allure and you will always feel ugly, and when time and age start showing, you will die a million deaths before they finally plant you. On one level, we all know this stuff already – it's been codified as myths, proverbs, clichés, bromides, epigrams, parables: the skeleton of every great story. The trick is keeping the truth up front in daily consciousness.[4]

Foster Wallace, though not a Christian, understood well the trap of forming our identity on something apart from God. If there is a glaring error that he made, it is that not all 'gods' are the same – he missed the uniqueness of Jesus Christ.

We need an identity that is secure, not transient; liberating, not enslaving. Part of the problem with seeking to form our identity online is that we know it fails both of these criteria, as the quote above makes clear. Jesus says, 'This is eternal life, that they know you the only true God, and Jesus Christ whom you have sent' (John 17:3). In John, eternal life is not some future state of blissful existence we must just wait for. It is the life of God that sustains us into eternity breaking into the present.

This life may not be fully realized until all creation is made new and God's glory fills the earth, but it comes to us now through a relationship with the eternal life-giving God, and his Son Jesus Christ. Jesus is uniquely the one who can offer it to us, because he is unique: he is the only one who has died for us to pay for our idolatry. In his death he takes on himself all of the consequences of our broken identities.

For those who seek their identity in popularity, Jesus was rejected by everyone, even his Father in heaven, so that we might have the unconditional acceptance we crave. For those who worship money and things and fear having nothing, Jesus died stripped of all possessions and worth so that we might receive the riches of God. For those who worship beauty and their image, Jesus the infinitely beautiful Bridegroom of heaven became cosmically ugly on the cross, 'marred, beyond human semblance' (Isaiah 52:14), so that we might be made beautiful in him.

This unique identity, offered freely but at great cost, is infinitely secure because it is sealed in Jesus' blood. It is infinitely liberating, given to us not because of anything we do but because of what he has done for us.

We started this chapter talking about René Descartes and the project of the Enlightenment that launched the modern world. The history is important because it reminds us of what is easy to forget. The ways we think about life, which seem obvious to us, haven't always been the ways people have thought about life. This is certainly true when it comes to the question of human identity, which has been thoroughly reimagined.

Part of the 'project' of the digital age – forming our identity online – takes up this project of reimagining who we are. But 'I tweet therefore I am' will always come up profoundly short. Descartes is famous for retreating to his room to seek certainty in the solitude. He tried making himself the certain point of reference by forgetting what had come before. We have sought to remember what has come before by going back to Geneva and John Calvin. Descartes isolated himself in his solitary room; we are pointing to the need to connect with God through Jesus Christ and to those around us in the world.

The irony of the modern self that was formed in isolation is that taking control of our own identity has left people unable to be alone. We need others, not to serve them but so that they can serve us. We need an audience to affirm us in our project to make ourselves the people we desperately want to be. This is one of the reasons social media is so attractive. It gives us the followers who can help us to be ourselves. Of course, we agree to help others to be themselves as well, so it isn't entirely selfish. The modern world is not beyond redemption. Perhaps a good practical step to take would be a backwards one. How might you build a regular practice of solitude and self-reflection into life? We aren't talking about running away from the world, but retreating in order to reorientate ourselves for life in the world. Perhaps you could adopt a daily or weekly practice of reflection and prayer where you actively leave digital technology aside, remembering who you are before God.

The aim of this backward step is a surer forwards one – one that is more confident of its direction and more secure of the ground on which it stands. Coming to God, turning from the idols of the world and knowing increasingly the life that he alone can give, sends us back to the world to re-engage in a way that doesn't use the world to define ourselves or depend on others to make us who we are.

One man who learned more truly who he was as he stepped back from the world was the German pastor Dietrich Bonhoeffer. Imprisoned in Nazi Germany for opposing Hitler's brutal regime, Bonhoeffer was sentenced to death. His life before prison was as a public figure and prominent academic. In prison, days before his execution and stripped of all he held dear, he contemplated his identity. The poem he wrote remains fiercely relevant for our digital age:

Who am I? This or the Other?
Am I one person today and tomorrow another?
Am I both at once? A hypocrite before others,
And before myself a contemptible woebegone weakling?

Or is something within me still like a beaten army
Fleeing in disorder from victory already achieved?
Who am I? They mock me, these lonely questions of mine.
Whoever I am, Thou knowest, O God, I am thine![5]

Questions for reflection

1. Reflect on your usage of social media. How frequently
   do you check Facebook or Twitter and how long do
   you spend on these and other social media platforms?
   What does this reveal to you?
2. What are the things you are tempted to form your
   identity on? A good way to diagnose this is to think
   about your 'screensaver' – where does your mind
   naturally drift when it is idle?
3. In what ways have you experienced the insecurity and
   enslavement of worshipping things that are not God?
4. How does knowing that Jesus took the consequences of
   your idolatry and so offers you totally secure acceptance
   change your perception of yourself?
5. As you find your identity in Christ, what bad online
   habits will you need to break? Think about negative
   behaviours you want to change; how can you involve
   others to help you?

The social network

'We lived on farms, then we lived in cities, and now we're gonna live on the Internet.' So spoke Sean Parker, playing the part of Mark Zuckerberg in the film, *The Social Network*. With 1.3 billion users worldwide, there is little doubt about the central part Facebook is playing in the realization of this vision. We will consider the Facebook phenomenon later in this chapter. But we cannot begin there. Facebook did not bring 'social' to the network; the 'social network' is really the Internet as a whole.

What should 'life on the Internet' look like? Should it even be lived there? What does it look like to let the gospel of Jesus Christ impact us in this area? Unfriend and log off, or log on and start a group? Most of us are aware that it should affect our usage more deeply than just the occasional Bible verse on our status update or the label 'Christian' on our profile (though that might be a start). But what should its effect be? That's what this chapter seeks to answer by exploring the social network story and rediscovering God's place in overcoming disconnection.

To begin, we need to go back to the start of the Internet. The Internet has its origins in the United States at the time of the Cold War. Every solution has its problem, often related to the problem it was seeking to solve. The particular issue that the Internet was invented to solve was the problem of military communication: how could American military commanders talk to missile operators in the event of a nuclear attack disabling their communications network?

The telephone network that the military relied on was highly centralized, with all phone calls being routed through a small number of exchanges. If one of these centres was destroyed by an attack, the US military command would have no way of communicating. Missile operators, with the power to launch a counter-attack almost immediately, would be left to determine for themselves how to respond.

Without their control the prospect of the situation turning into an all-out nuclear conflict was one that senior military personnel considered all too likely. The urgent need, presented in a memo to President John F. Kennedy in the early 1960s, was for a new kind of communications network.

At the time, Paul Baran was an engineer working for the RAND Corporation, a defence research organization. As early as the 1960s he raised his concern about the weakness of the centralized network and in 1962 he wrote a memorandum outlining an alternative: 'On Distributed Communications Networks' (the title wasn't meant to be inspiring!). Unlike a centralized network, or connection of smaller centralized networks (often referred to as 'decentralized'), a distributed network is not susceptible to being incapacitated in the same way. Even if a nuclear attack knocked out one or more points in the network, there are multiple paths that can be followed from one point to another. Gone is the hierarchy of authority, and the centres of control. In a distributed network

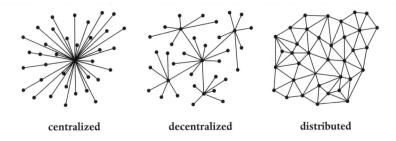

centralized   decentralized   distributed

every node is an equally important part of the community: welcome to the social network!

It was one thing to dream up such a network, however, and another thing to build one that could work in practice. The American military turned to the emerging computing community for help.

In many ways, this was not a natural partnership. The centralized command structures of the military mirrored the existing telecommunications network that was causing such a headache. The computing fraternity, on the other hand, was an open community where anyone who wanted to join was welcomed to collaborate. Lots of its members were graduate students, and they brought with them the 'hacker' culture – a term first used in the model railway club at MIT (Massachusetts Institute of Technology). Here the values were not the strict order and discipline of the military, but creativity, collaboration and radical openness.

Among this group, circulated documents were not 'memoranda' but 'requests for comments' that were intentionally lacking in authority in order to encourage further contribution and development. Fifty years later, the anti-authoritarian principles of open collaboration and 'perpetual beta' (all work remains 'work in progress') continue to be core values of the computing community: 'We reject kings, presidents and voting. We believe in rough consensus and running code.'[1]

This is the community that in 1976 sent the first cross-network transmissions using 'internet' protocol from a beer garden. This is the community that created the Internet in its image and, through social media, has invited the world to join.

The key point is this: the revolution in human connectivity wasn't added to the Internet at the start of the twenty-first century. It was hard-wired in the design of the network from the beginning.

Overcoming disconnection

The communication problems the US military faced in the Cold War might have catalysed early investment in the development of the Internet, but they are part of a bigger story of overcoming disconnection. In 2012 Facebook reached 1 billion users, a truly staggering number for an online community that only began in 2004.

To mark the significance of this moment in its history, film director Alejandro Innurito was called in to produce a video that would present Facebook's profile to its world. It is entitled 'The Things That Connect Us' (have a look online) and combines some stunning cinematography with deep philosophy (relying heavily on our friend 'the digger', whom we met in chapter 1). In the film, there is no computer, smartphone or Internet connection anywhere in sight.

In the video the essence of Facebook is nothing technological. It is about people, and how they are connected in relationship. Facebook is compared to chairs, bridges, doorbells, a great nation (you can imagine how many YouTube spoof videos have been made out of this!). The idea is that these things connect people and allow us to open up and share our ideas, our time, our love.

As the film ends, the screen goes black before 'Facebook' appears, shining brightly in the darkness. The closing words underline the point that is being communicated: 'The universe is vast and dark and makes us wonder if we are alone, so maybe the reason that we make all of these things is to remind us that we are not.'

The deep human problem we are pointed to is isolation. Technology has enabled us to grasp something of the scope of the universe and our place in it (think about the photographs we have seen of the earth from space that have only been possible for sixty years). We have been made aware of how small human beings are and how little we know and control.

This can be exciting – the universe is beautiful and there is much to explore. But it can also be terrifying – if we don't know where the earth belongs, how can we know where we belong? The old structures of life and social institutions are perhaps not as stable as we once assumed they were. The only place we can be sure we belong is together. The promise of a relational network is that space and time can't keep us apart. Wherever we are, whatever time it is, if we are part of the network, the network knows where we are and we are not alone. The light of the network overcomes the darkness.

It is not only Facebook that tells this story. It is part of the wider historical narrative of the modern world, stunningly portrayed by director Danny Boyle in the opening ceremony of the 2012 London Olympics. The pre-modern green and pleasant land of England was portrayed as a place of traditional values and community life, but the naivety quickly vanishes, along with the light, as the dark days of the Industrial Revolution come over the land.

The scene is pandemonium – industry fills the darkness as workers are forced to operate in time with the drumbeat of progress. It is a scene of control and power and pride: wealthy elites profiting from the work and ensuring order, as the drums of progress seem to beat the stone-faced workers to death. Only the world wars of the twentieth century could cause the industry to pause.

The work of the many was not in vain, however. From the unity of their labour came a strength of community represented in the shining Olympic rings. From the time of reflection on the horrors of war came the cultural revolution of the 1960s – light and colour emerged from the darkness of Blake's 'satanic mills'.

The scene is brighter, but the historical narrative hasn't yet reached its fulfilment. That comes when the colours of the 1960s reappear fifty years later. Dance music replaced the drums, and the co-ordinated action of the factories was turned into a much happier harmony, centring on a romance where a couple were brought together in love, made possible by instant messaging.

This new world is the connected world, networked along with the 80,000 people in the stadium. Each held one of the LED lights that created some incredible visual effects and were used to spell out the message that is the gospel of the networked world. As Sir Tim Berners-Lee, the inventor of the World Wide Web, was revealed at the heart of the scene, light blazed out of his computer screen and the network of lights showed the message: from one angle, 'This is for ever', from another, 'This is for everyone'.

This is the story of connectivity that is shaping life in the digital age. A new 'distributed' network of light and life has emerged from the old 'centralized' network of darkness and death. There is no more disconnection, because this new world is open to all!

Life online

In an interview fifteen years after the invention of the World Wide Web, Tim Berners-Lee spoke of how it had evolved.[2] He expressed delight at the way the Web had become an international network, a medium of communication that facilitated human interaction and community across the globe. His vision of 'a collaborative medium, a place where we all meet and read and write', was being fulfilled.

This evolution is sometimes described in terms of a transition from the early 'go to' web, which was a source of information, to the new and improved version, 'Web 2.0'. Can you feel the progress? In 'Web 2.0' the network has become a new society, an interactive community with embedded values, a place where anyone can belong and where everyone has something to contribute to our life together, sharing their ideas and images and experiences.

The Internet has become the place where we keep up with our family, reconnect with our friends, pursue romantic relationships. But more than replicating our offline relationships in a new mode, the Internet has the power to take us beyond ourselves as the means by which we join in relationship to the whole world.

Of course, there will still be challenges to confront; even the sunniest techno-optimists willingly recognize that. But if we live on the Internet, the promise is that we live in the constant peace of a new global community. If we follow Google's vision in *The New Digital Age*, the best-selling book by two senior figures at the company, we will be optimistic that this new connectivity can be a factor in uniting the world, overcoming political and religious disagreement, improving education, solving environmental challenges, and elevating human life to a new level of connected existence.

The speed of transition may seem rapid, but it shouldn't be overstated. Numbers of users do not tell the whole story, and it is still too early to discern the nature of the Internet's social influence. Much is new, but much is old too. The relational impulse that is powering the growth of the Internet is as old as creation. People will always find new ways of living together, for we are relational beings made in the image of an eternally relational God.

For most people, the reality of social media is not nearly as elevated as some of the discussion surrounding its pros and cons. In fact, it is in the more ordinary things that the real blessings are experienced. There is surely much to be thankful for in the digital connections of daily life: it is incredible to be able to keep up with family in different parts of the world. It is fruitful to collaborate and learn together as we share online. It is good to rejoice with those who rejoice and mourn with those who mourn. It is encouraging to receive messages from friends in places that we cannot be. It is wonderful to have a week away from home and yet have fun sharing video messages back and forth. Where there is good in the social network, and there is much, let us rejoice and be glad in it.

Hopefully, by now you are starting to get a sense of how social media networks fit into the wider story of the Internet and its place in the modern world. In many ways, social media is an expression of the Internet coming into its own – less an innovation added to the Internet as the way in which the values present in the network could be fully expressed.

So far we have focused on Facebook, but of course it is not the only social media network, nor was it the first. MySpace was there before Mark Zuckerberg opened Facebook to the Web. LinkedIn currently has the lion's share of the professional social network market. Twitter is the #micro option. Flickr and Instagram focus on photos, Pinterest on shared interests and projects. Medium is a pleasing middle way between a social network and a blog. Napster was there early and concentrated on sharing music, but then there was Spotify. Other platforms are popular in different countries and languages; Sina Weibo (a hybrid of Facebook and Twitter) has 500 million users in China.

This plethora of social media sites shouldn't downplay the remarkable feat that Facebook has achieved in recruiting 1.3 billion people to its network in only ten years. But it should cause us to pause for thought before we assume that Facebook is a permanent feature of life that has solved the problem of human disconnection. When the company began listing on the stock market, it allowed investors to act as a jury on that score, and they are still trying to decide.

It is still worth asking why Facebook has attracted so many more users than other platforms. In his book, *iGods*,[3] Craig Detweiler suggests this is because the values embedded in Facebook matched the values of the people they were seeking to connect with their network.

Compared to MySpace, Facebook's design was clean and minimalist, communicating a sense of calm confidence. The limit to personalization meant that everyone's profile could look good, taking away some of the design preferences that people love to have, but actually find crippling. The values of openness, integrity, personal endorsement and acceptance filled Facebook, as they did other social media networks. But as Steve Jobs did at Apple, Facebook's attention to detail carefully embedded these values in the minutiae of the site in ways that make Facebook a desirable place to be.

Or should that be *made* Facebook a desirable place to be? Like investors, users can be a fickle bunch. Frustrations with the use of targeted advertising and modifications to Facebook's user privacy agreement have raised the question as to whether the network could fall out of favour as quickly as it fell into it. Time will tell.

A love/hate relationship

As much as we can say 'yes' to social networks and love to use them, they are at the same time the social networks we love to hate. There is a growing trend of social media scepticism in books and newspaper articles and even in our online news feeds. This evening we are working in a café next to London's Barbican Centre and a conversation has just started at the next table: 'The problem with Twitter is . . .' How would you continue?

For all the good that the social network brings, it is not hard to see why we have mixed feelings. Twitter fills our newsfeed with adverts. We have had too many of those already. Facebook does the same, targeting the preferences that its algorithms have discerned from our posts, our place, our peers.

The conversations online can often be thin, and we sometimes wonder how much the 'likes' are actually worth. It is nice to have lots of 'followers', and satisfying when we get a 'retweet', but we know how long it takes to hit 'favourite'. The approval it conveys is not always very meaningful.

There is a deeper concern too about the nature of friendship being changed for the worse. A friend recently told us of his struggle with alcoholism, which left him feeling isolated and let down by those he had thought were there for him. Plenty of people had 'liked' his status updates. But when he posted asking for help, no-one stepped out of the network and into his flat to help him. No-one picked up the phone to call. Of course, there are other examples of people who have found incredible help and support online in times of need, but the concern persists that friendship must be deeper than online communities alone will allow.

What should we do with the inner sceptic when it comes to social media, and the way our relationships are being shaped? When we hear the voice of the doubters without or within, should we just 'keep calm and carry on'? Or should we take these concerns more seriously and adopt a deeper scepticism about the premise of networked sociality itself?

Sherry Turkle is a psychologist, TED speaker, and the concerned author of *Alone Together*, a book highlighting some of the potentially harmful effects of a socially networked existence.[4] Rather than connecting us, she argues, the social Web is bringing increased fragmentation to our lives. We have moved from conversation to connection, from talking to texting, from solitude to isolation, from interdependent to interconnected.

What do you think? It seems to us that her objections cannot be easily dismissed. The promise of the social network, the promise to be the light in the darkness that brings life to the world, isn't a promise it can deliver.

The ambiguity of our social media experience testifies to that. The promise is that when we are part of the network we are always at home, but the reality we often experience is of being everywhere and nowhere, distracted from life at home by the urge to check our feed. The promise is that when we are part of the network our voice will always be heard, but the reality we often experience is an anxiety that no-one is really listening. Sometimes we need to send a tweet out into the ether in order just to check. Waiting for the 'like' or retweet just to know that someone is there. The promise of the network is that we will never be alone, but the reality we often experience is of heightened self-awareness and feeling as lonely as ever.

The resolution to the love / hate tension is found in revisiting the story of the social network. Here's the problem: the network that brings so much good with it cannot bear the weight that the world is looking to assign to it. The world is looking for a light in the darkness and looking to the Internet to provide it.

Seeing the network as the answer actually turns the network into the problem. This is the pattern of idolatry that we saw in the previous chapter. A good thing that is made into an ultimate thing is an idol that cannot bear the weight. When the network becomes ultimate, 'connection' becomes all-important, 'sharing' becomes essential, our life is reduced to our place in a global grid where 'I am who I am connected to'. The network, if we assign it the place of ultimacy that only the God of love can hold, will, in the words of the writer David Foster Wallace, 'eat you alive'. The grander the narrative and the greater the promise, the bigger the failure.

The social network is an incredible thing which can bring real blessing to our lives, but the blessing is always dependent on the God who made all things good. If it is life and light that we are looking for, the person to look to is him.

A deeper connection

People love and thrive in relationship, and so of course we enjoy new ways to talk and interact and share and encourage and learn together. But the Internet cannot give us the secure place in the world that we crave. Of course it can't: after all, it is only a vast network of computers.

Remember how the Facebook video ended: 'The universe is vast and dark and makes us wonder if we are alone, so maybe the reason that we make all of these things is to remind us that we are not.' The dark universe is the world without God; it is the world that leaves us wondering if we are alone. But there is another story, a better story:

> The heavens declare the glory of God,
>   and the sky above proclaims his handiwork.
> Day to day pours out speech,
>   and night to night reveals knowledge . . .
> Their voice goes out through all the earth,
>   and their words to the end of the world.
> (Psalm 19:1–4)

The universe is not vast and dark and empty. It loudly declares that God exists. It sings in praise of his glory, a glory that he has made known in the one who entered the darkness of history and shone as the light of life: 'The Word became flesh and dwelt among us, and we have seen his glory, glory as of the only Son from the Father, full of grace and truth' (John 1:14).

The world's longing for connection is a desire to have a place in the world in relationship with others. But that longing can only be satisfied when relationship with others is also a relationship with God. The Bible describes secure relationships in terms of covenants. They are relationships built on the security of mutual commitments and promises. As theologian Michael Horton puts it:

> This covenantal relationality is essential to our being
> human. There are not first autonomous individuals who
> then may (or may not) enter into covenantal relations.
> From the moment of conception, each of us is already
> a participant in the web of human histories, relationships,
> genetics, and nurture that condition our personal
> identity.[5]

Horton is saying that relational connection with others and with God is hard-wired into our very being. We are made for secure relationships. People are not independent individuals who overcome their isolation by plugging into a network. We are relational to our core.

Feelings of isolation, of being lost and alone in the darkness of the universe, come not because we are alone but because we close our eyes to the presence of God and the needs of others. The call of Christ is to view the world through new eyes. To turn from a misplaced trust in the half-light of digital connectivity, to see his glory and receive his grace. As he calls us to follow, he calls us into a renewed relationship with him that flows outwards in love to others.

Social networks are good but they don't hold the ultimate answers. They are not the source of light in a dark universe. Christ calls us to belong in his family, receiving and sharing his love. It is as part of this community of life and light, serving others and reaching out in love, that the sense of isolation loses its grip. This is the wonder of life together in relationship with God. Not so much connection as communion, a word that speaks not just of sharing carefully chosen information but a true sharing of ourselves.

As we come to the end of this chapter, it is important to recognize that every grand vision must land in the world. In our digital age, the media presence of the Internet can seem far more attractive than the real presence of Christ among his people.

Dietrich Bonhoeffer in his book *Life Together* describes the wonder of the ordinary life of people brought together by God in local congregations, worshipping together and serving one another and the world. The church is far from perfect. Networks where we can choose our neighbours before we love our neighbours are surely easier places to spend time. But the true light of the world, Jesus Christ, is present among his people. Bonhoeffer's words are good ones to reflect on: 'The bright day of Christian community dawns wherever the early morning mists of dreamy visions are lifting.'[6]

I have seen this light breaking in through the mist many times at Inspire church in London where I (Pete) am a pastor. One week there was a situation where a woman had a painful conversation with another church member. She was upset, and part of that was right, though, as is often the case, there was fault on both sides. The next we heard, she was thinking of leaving the church. She had no problem with the church itself but didn't want to be around the other person. It was the real-life equivalent of 'unfriending' someone. People talked to her, and after some persuasion she spoke to the person. He said sorry and the relationship was greatly strengthened as a result.

It's a small, unspectacular example, but that makes it all the more important. Interactions like this are so vital for our growth and for the strength of our friendships. In a world where we can unfriend someone and they won't even know, it is too easy to opt out of community because it is the path of least resistance. But the easy life is not the same as the good life.

The good life, where the light breaks through, will be found in the simple but grace-filled interactions of a community on and offline: rejoicing together, weeping together, worshipping together, serving one another, forgiving one another, bearing with one another, praying for each other, correcting each other and comforting each other, for in doing so we fulfil the law of love (Romans 13:10).

Questions

1. What are the benefits of social networks that you are grateful for? Why not pause and spend some time thanking God for them?
2. In your life, how do you see the inadequacy of making social networks your primary place of community? Perhaps think of times/ways that social networks have replaced meeting with someone you would otherwise have seen in person.
3. What are the ways you are tempted to make Facebook/Twitter/other social networks 'ultimate'? How many times a day do you check Facebook and what does this tell you?
4. How does it reassure you to know that you have a Father in heaven and that by faith he is always in communion with you and you with him?
5. Compare the quality and quantity of your connection with the social network with the intentional time you devote to deepening relationship with God in prayer, Bible reading and corporate worship. What might you want to change in light of this?
6. How does your life show the priority of the ordinary local church as God's community?
7. We are made for life together. If you have found that this chapter has started you thinking, who else can you bring into the conversation?

Real time

In Boulder, Colorado, in the National Institute of Standards and Technology, there is the most precise clock in the world. The Ytterbium Atomic Clock (YAC for short) is so precise that it wasn't possible to measure its precision until recently, when a second version was built!

Apparently YAC is about 10 billion times more accurate than a quartz wristwatch. The Swiss need not worry: it weighs more than a tonne and becomes very inaccurate if it is moved!

Time is a key consideration in modern technology. Many commentators write about the perceived quickening pace of modern life. Richard Powers, the science fiction author, writes about a disease he calls 'real time':

> In real time every second counts, every minute must be
> maximised. Since we cannot stop the escaping moments, we
> have our machines give us the next best thing: two moments,
> crammed into one. Split screen. Multitasking. Mobile Wireless
> voicemail message forwarding. RSS feeds. Picture-in-picture.
> We need miss nothing. In fact we can't . . . In real time we live

in two minds, three tenses, and four continents at once and buy back the bits lost in transition with frequent flyer miles. In short we have grown so good at mastering time that nanoseconds now weigh heavy on our hands.[1]

Just as well then that we have the Ytterbium Atomic Clock to measure all those nanoseconds we are losing!

Just down the road from where we are writing this in London is Clerkenwell. Arguably the most significant invention of the Industrial Revolution was not the steam engine, or the telegraph, but the clock. In the mid to late eighteenth century, Clerkenwell was the clock-making centre of the Western world – a kind of Silicon Valley of its day. Within fifty years many households and businesses had clocks. Within a hundred years almost everyone in London was able to 'watch' the time on a small clock they carried on their person.

With clocks and watches so widely available, a new context for life was born. Try to imagine what it was like before these time-measuring devices became widespread. For thousands of years human timekeeping had been a set of habits marking the passing of time by reference to simple measurements – the place of the sun in the sky or the length of shadows. Then the sundial made time-measurement based on the movement of the sun more accurate. But when mechanical clocks clicked into gear, much changed.

In particular there are two changes that we think are key to understanding our digital age. First, time began to be seen as exclusively chronological – a purely linear progression with a definite historic beginning and end. Second, time started to be seen as a commodity.

If time is linear, with a definite beginning and end, progressing from one to the other with each tick of the clock, then it is not long before you realize there is only so much of it to go around! Consequently time has become not just a context for life but something we need to 'use', 'spend' and be careful not to 'waste'. Lorenzo Simpson captures both of these elements when he writes, 'The clock as a representation of time as linear, as irreversible, as the bearer of the irretrievable, is a key to the technological phenomenon.'[2]

We will take these two elements in turn: time as a straight line and time as a commodity, and see how the gospel gives us both a 'yes' and a 'no' to them. By reframing time as God's gift to be wisely stewarded, we will ease some of the excessive pressures of 'real time' while leaving a place to heed the Bible's call to make the 'best use of time' (see Colossians 4:5).

Time as an arrow to the future

It might seem strange to question the modern view of time as a straight line. What else would it be? But in ancient society, time was also viewed in cycles. It was marked by the repetition of festivals that noted key milestones every year and which were repeated. True, there would be a sense of the passing of time, but then a new day or year would start and the cycle repeated. Now we view time exclusively as a straight line, starting at a particular point and ending at a point but, crucially, with development and improvement at each successive stage. Time is an arrow to the future.

It is striking how much our view of time is bound up with our view of progress. The new is thought of as automatically better than the old. We have noted some of this already in chapter 2 and particularly how it is reinforced by a numerical way of labelling things.

We count versions of books or products, and because we count up (Windows 9 to Windows 10), we assume the next version is better. This is not to deny that sometimes the upgrades *are* better, but better against what set of criteria? Many of us have experienced the frustration of an upgrade that we find out is worse than the previous version. It is what we called in chapter 2 the assumption of progress.

What if we named things differently, what if we decided to call the versions after (for example) animals? Would Windows Buffalo automatically feel better than the Windows Wombat?! 'Ah,' you say, 'that is just what Apple do!' Well yes, and at the same time no. Even the animal names are numbered: 'Mac OS X v10.0 Cheetah' or 'Mac OS X v10.6 Snow Leopard'. The numbers and the perception of progress are difficult to resist.

Our arrow view of time also crops up in the story that we tell about the past. We have the Dark Ages from the fifth century onwards (darkness implying a kind of ignorance and immorality), then we have the Middle Ages taking us up to the fifteenth century (you see it is getting lighter), then light breaks in at the Enlightenment, bringing the modern scientific movement and new freedom from overbearing institutions.

All of this gives the impression of steady improvement and an evolution in human thought, intelligence and morality. (This story rather awkwardly airbrushes out the unfortunate truth that the twentieth century was the bloodiest in human history.) If I accept this view, then when some new technology is released it must be good for me just because it is new. The new is better than the old. Some, notably C. S. Lewis, call this 'chronological snobbery', 'the uncritical acceptance of the intellectual climate of our own age and the assumption that whatever has gone out of date is on that count discredited'.[3]

It is striking how this chronological snobbery uncritically underpins our thinking in the West. Here is the logic:

- We are the most technologically developed culture on earth.
- Since time is an arrow to the future, that means we are at the head of the curve.
- Therefore our decisions (about morality, society, technology) are the most 'progressive'.
- So, if other people / countries / cultures disagree, it is because they are lagging behind (but in time they will catch up and probably agree with us).

These assumptions are now so deeply embedded that they often go unnoticed. But if we pause and reflect for a moment, such beliefs should make us feel very uncomfortable. They mask a deep-seated pride and a form of cultural imperialism that has a dark past.

We need to be balanced here and not commit the opposite error of resisting change just because it is change. The Bible does not hark back to some golden era and neither should we. Progress is not a myth. There are historical developments and improvements. However, the uncritical assumption of progress is our modern blind spot and this is what we need to question.

God's timeline

In many senses the Bible's view of history is also an arrow. In fact, the modern story of history as an arrow to the future was borrowed (and adapted) from Christianity. There is a definite beginning and there will be a definite end. True, there are some cyclical elements to history, particularly the important festivals in the Old and New Testaments that are milestones for remembering God's actions in history. But these cycles exist within a larger framework of the beginning and the end that history is heading for.

However, we need to be careful of our use of the word 'end'. There is the 'end' of ceasing to exist and the 'end' of reaching a goal.

The secular view of history sees it as heading for a hard stop. In thermodynamics the discovery of increasing entropy in the universe has led to talk of heat death, when everything has become so spread out that there are no more energy differences and the universe stops. It may be a long way off, but under this view the universe and time itself will one day grind to a halt. Therefore time is limited.

However, God reveals that the end of history is not its finish but its goal. The Bible draws on rich metaphors to make this point: a wedding day which is the goal of an engagement is perhaps its most vivid. The metaphor is also instructive. When a couple gets married it is not the finish of the relationship. In many ways it is the start. Equally no couple gets engaged to stay engaged: there is only so much wedding admin ('wedmin') that anyone can stomach! You get engaged to get married. The engagement ends but the relationship continues. So we are told that the world is waiting 'with eager longing' (Romans 8:19) for its future 'consummation'. It won't be a dead end to history; it will be a new beginning, a doorway to the future.

C. S. Lewis captures this memorably in the final book of the Narnia series, *The Last Battle*:

And as He [Aslan] spoke, He no longer looked to them like a lion; but the things that began to happen after that were so great and beautiful that I cannot write them. And for us this is the end of all the stories, and we can most truly say that they all lived happily ever after. But for them it was only the beginning of the real story. All their life in this world and all their adventures in Narnia had only been the cover and the title page: now at last they were beginning Chapter One of

the Great Story which no one on earth has read: which
goes on for ever: in which every chapter is better than
the one before.[4]

The second key aspect of the timeline is that it is God's
timeline and not ours. God is the prime mover in history and
he is in control. This is not to say that we are written out of
the story; far from it. God's story is one that graciously
includes us. We are vital to it as a story of what he has done
to create us, redeem us and bring us into his New Creation.
But one of the dangers of technology is the way that it gives
us a device to write God out of the story and put ourselves in
his place.

Think about how we narrate when the day starts. In the
Hebrew way of thinking, the day did not start in the morning
but started at sunset. That is why Genesis repeats the phrase,
'and there was evening and morning, the first/second/third
... day'. It is a perception-changing truth when we realize
that as we go to sleep, having to rest because we are creatures,
the Creator is at work through the night. 'He who watches
over Israel never slumbers or sleeps' (Psalm 121:4 NLT).

When we wake up we are not the prime movers in the
world. God has been at work, and his gracious invitation is
for us to co-work with him in the 'good works, which God
prepared beforehand, that we should walk in them' (Ephesians
2:10). As our heads hit the pillow, God is still there sustaining
the cosmos by his word of power (Hebrews 1:3), causing the
rain to fall and the crops to grow.

One of the illusions of technology is that while we sleep
and rest, our work continues through the technology we have
made. On one level this is true. I switch the dishwasher on, or
set my laptop to back up data, or have my phone downloading
an update, and I don't need to be 'doing' anything. But just as

using a tractor to work the field can mask the reality that we are still dependent on God to make the crops grow, so having devices whirring away in the background does not mean that we are now suddenly in control. We are still just as dependent on God as ever. All that has happened is that we have added another layer that, if we are not careful, veils our true need for dependence on him.

Technology can, when misused, give a false self-sufficiency. It can mask the reality that behind our innovations we are still totally dependent on God. As a consequence we too easily retell the story of history with God written out and ourselves shifted into his place as the prime movers and heroes of the piece. In fact that is just what the Enlightenment did. It took the Christian view of history – time as an arrow to God's future. It changed the main character – time as an arrow to humanity's future! Technology's story is often told as being the way humanity will bring about the future.

To draw things together, here are two key insights to 'real time' – time as it really is:

1. Time is not a straight line heading for a finish. God is taking the cosmos towards its goal. In one sense this goal is the end of time; in another sense it is just the beginning.
2. The timeline is God's and not ours. We are graciously part of his-story, but we need to watch out for the ways technology can be used to try to write him out and put us centre stage.

Time as a commodity

If we think time is limited and if we think we are in control of time, then it becomes a commodity. Economists talk of a resource becoming a commodity when it fulfils two criteria. First, it must be a scarce resource – there is only a limited amount to go round. Second, it must be a private good – something that can be owned and possessed.

Notice how the two wrong views of time analysed above fit these criteria. We talk of 'spending time', 'taking time', 'wasting time' and 'maximizing time'. Many commentators argue that time has become the most important commodity of the modern world. Have you ever heard someone lament being 'cash rich and time poor'? Have you felt that way yourself? Have you heard the phrase 'I've just bought/won myself an hour'? We all feel like we're trading in the time market.

Part of time's importance can be seen in the values by which we assess technology. Often the great values we measure things by and look for in our technology are the virtues of:

- productivity – amount produced over time
- efficiency – time and energy expended in output
- speed – distance over time.

Again it all relates back to the way that our story frames time. If we set time up as a commodity then of course productivity, efficiency and speed are key. You see a computer processor advert that tells you it is 'faster than conventional processors'. The advertisers don't even need to tell you why that means it is better. That argument has already been won.

Are we then advocating a go-slow movement? Are productivity, efficiency and speed important at all? Again the gospel of Jesus Christ says both 'yes' and 'no'. Yes, time is important and the Bible does call us to 'make the best use of time' (see Colossians 4:5). Productivity, efficiency and speed have their place. Laziness is not a vice condoned in Scripture:

Go to the ant, O sluggard;
   consider her ways, and be wise.
Without having any chief,
   officer, or ruler,
she prepares her bread in summer
   and gathers her food in harvest.
How long will you lie there, O sluggard?
   When will you arise from your sleep?
(Proverbs 6:6–9)

But no, efficiency and productivity are not the supreme values in the world. We need to get them in perspective by reframing time in the right way as a gift to be stewarded.

Time as a gift to be stewarded

There is a website called 'Death Clock' which claims to tell you when you are going to die. You enter your date of birth, gender, how positive you are feeling about life, how overweight you are and whether you are a smoker, and hit 'Check your death clock'. Then a clock counting down to your death appears. It seems to us that all the anxiety caused by going through that rigmarole probably knocks ten years off your life regardless of the result!

In contrast the psalmist prays, 'Teach us to number our days that we may get a heart of wisdom' (Psalm 90:12). He does not go to some calculator to number his days, but to God. What a vital prayer this is for our culture.

God gives us our time as a gift. It is never a gift we possess absolutely. That is partly why none of us can be sure how long we will live for, nor do we know when history will reach its goal. By withholding that information from us, God ensures that we have to receive time by faith, trusting that he knows best and he has our best interests at heart.

But we need to add to this our stewardship of time. God does not just gift us time as a lump that we can divide up any way we see fit. He is far more specific than that. God determines allotted periods and the boundaries of our lives (Acts 17:26). He decides the length of our lives (Psalm 90:12). He determines the structure of our week – six days of work and one day of rest (Exodus 20:9–11; Deuteronomy 5:13). He even carefully apportions the challenges we face each day (Matthew 6:34).

So stewarding is not about a frantic struggle to squeeze out of life the most that we can. Stewarding time is about ordering our lives properly according to God's divine purpose and plan.

Let's apply this in two areas: anxiety and rest.

Anxiety

Often we make ourselves anxious because we try to load tomorrow's challenges into today. Issues coming up at work, the people we have to meet, the shopping we need to do. This causes a kind of mental overload. We are having to deal not only with what we are doing now, but also what is coming up. Think of when a computer gets overheated and you hear its fan whirring. You realize the problem is that you have too many programs opened. It is the human equivalent of that.

Technology can exacerbate the problem. As well as loading tomorrow's problems into today, we have texts, tweets, status updates and emails all flooding in, beeping and buzzing in our pockets. Because our devices can run apps simultaneously we try to live simultaneously. But multitasking can make the problem worse by increasing our mental burden. In addition many studies show it costs time rather than saves time.[5] Many times we do it because it gives us the illusion of efficiency, but rarely does it actually save time and often it stresses us out.

Of course there are tasks that technology can automate. Travel, production, calculation . . . the list could go on. We are not denying that technology does save a lot of time and for that we should be thankful. But we need to dig deeper. If technology is saving us so much time, why are we so stressed, anxious and rushed?

Matthew 6:34 reminds us that because God apportions our time, 'sufficient for the day is its own trouble'. We can reduce anxiety by trusting God with the tasks he has given us to do today and in the now, and not worrying about things he has deferred for later. It is an act of faith to leave tomorrow in his hands. He has the wisdom to know what we can cope with and what we can't. Prayer is vital. In prayer we can entrust whatever is not for the now to the sovereign Lord. In prayer we ask for daily grace for the tasks God puts before us and for the understanding to know the things to leave in God's hand for another time.

Similarly with multitasking. It is an act of faith to acknowledge our limitations. You are not a computer. You are limited in how many tasks you can do at the same time. There is freedom in acknowledging your limits. Try doing things sequentially rather than simultaneously. You may feel that your task will take longer, but does it really? The chances are that it will take the same time (or less) and the quality will be higher. Alongside these benefits you will probably find your stress reduced.

Likewise, are you distracted? Do you find yourself talking to someone but your mind wanders because your phone buzzes in your pocket? Do your children or friends complain that they struggle to keep your attention because you are constantly looking at texts and emails? Of course it is not wrong to have your phone on vibrate. But do you really need to receive every message the moment it comes in?

Part of the way our digital age works is by FOMO: 'fear of missing out'. But the irony is that our fear of missing out is often what causes us to miss out! We miss out on what is right in front of our eyes. It is striking that Steve Jobs was very strict on limiting his family's use of iPhones around the house. Similarly Chris Anderson, the editor of *Wired*, has a blanket ban on using smartphones during family times.[6] Both were fearful of the impact of being distracted by devices and not really present in their relationships.

So why not think about the times you could switch on by switching off? Would you be better at listening to your friends or your children if your smartphone were off? Would your meetings at work be better if people weren't looking at emails under the table? Would you get more out of church if you weren't looking at Facebook during the sermon? Whatever application is appropriate, we could learn a lot from the prayer, 'O Lord, wherever I am, help me to be fully present.'

Rest

Part of the pattern God has ingrained in the world is a pattern of rest. He could have made us so that we never need sleep, or food. That would have been more efficient! But in his wisdom he has given us clear limits. These limits are not arbitrary. They are there to remind us that we are creatures, not the Creator. They are also there to remind us that we are *Homo adorans* – people of worship.

For centuries in the West, rest has been understood as being inseparably linked to worship. That understanding has shifted in the past thirty years. Making Sunday a day of rest and a day for the gathering of God's people was not accidental. The gathering of church together in communion before God is what rest is about. Think of the word 'recreation': re-creation. It implies renewal, not just the absence of work. The idea is that we stop working to be renewed in the image of our creator (Colossians 3:10). More often than not, today rest is understood purely in terms of leisure. But could it be that the restlessness we feel despite all our 'rest' is because we are not being renewed?

Weariness is different from tiredness because it is not something that sleep can fix. It is a tiredness of the heart, a sense of running low on emotional and spiritual resources. The call to remember the Sabbath brings with it Jesus' famous call, 'Come to me, all you who are weary and burdened, and I will give you rest. Take my yoke upon you and learn from me, for I am gentle and humble in heart' (Matthew 11:28–29 NIV).

Biblical rest is an absence of work so that we can give special attention to God and his people. Yes, worship is also an 'all of life' activity (Romans 12:1–2), but that is not to deny something significant about corporate worship as we gather together to hear God's Word, to encourage one another in prayer and song, and to enjoy the Lord's Supper together.

How do you view rest? As just the absence of work, or as something richer? What is the focus of your weekend? What is it that you think will refresh you ready for another week?

Martin Luther had a young and gifted friend called Philip Melanchthon. Melanchthon was prone to being too busy and feeling stressed. One day when Luther visited Philip, the younger man was wearied with overwork and weighed down with worry. As Philip poured out his anxieties and worries to his mentor, Luther gently said to him, 'May Philip cease to rule the world!' That advice is still relevant for many of us in our digital world.

Submitting to God's sovereign ordering of time as a gift to be stewarded according to his pattern is still the path of peace and rest today.

Questions

1. How would you rate your life, from too lazy to too busy? What lies behind your assessment? (For example, if you are too busy, why do you feel too busy?)
2. Are you too busy? If so, is it because you can't say no or don't say no?
3. How does seeing time as a gift to be wisely stewarded challenge your answers to questions 1 or 2?
4. What are the ways that you buy into the view that speed/efficiency/productivity are what really matter? Think about how you evaluate your week. On what basis do you decide whether you have had a good or a bad week?
5. When was the last time you turned off all your devices (phone/computer)? How did you feel?
6. What are the particular things that cause you anxiety and how do you try to use technology to cope rather than taking it to God? (For example, through escapism on YouTube, validation on Facebook, clearing your inbox to feel in control.)
7. Do you feel time-anxiety? If so, what do you think is behind this?
8. What is your pattern of rest? What part do God and his people have in your rest?

Virtual sex

Back in 2014, a teenage girl who sexted a topless selfie to her boyfriend received a police caution for distributing an indecent image of a child. Because he had the picture she sent on his phone, her boyfriend also received a caution for possession of child pornographic images. Both the girl and her boyfriend were warned by police that they risked being put on the sex offenders' register.[1]

The news story is a parable for our time: the loss of innocence in the pursuit of liberty. The real dangers of something labelled 'harmless fun'. Momentary choices that have long-term consequences. The story is about technology and its impact on sex.

We are so used to it that it hardly seems insightful to say that the landscape of sex is changing rapidly with technological advancements. Some of the changes may shock us: the speed at which old norms seem to have broken down, the huge increase in pornography, the new phenomenon of sexting (sexual interaction through text), websites devoted to facilitating adulterous relationships. Some of the developments may escape our notice: the growth of the image and the steady sexualization of advertising. Some of the changes may be a blessing, like the unmasking of damaging sexual taboos, or perhaps we could include love-matches made through online sites or dating forums.

But it's not only the 'how' of sexual interaction that is changing. The sex industry is growing, sexual habits and perceptions are changing, sexual expression is morphing, sexualization is affecting people at younger ages, sexual identity is shifting . . . the list could go on.

As with so many of the areas we are exploring in this book, one of the great challenges is getting our bearings. Change is often hard, but not all change is bad. How do we filter the good from the bad? How do we decide between what we want to say 'yes' to and what we need to say 'no' to?

In this chapter we will consider the digital story of sex and see that while it has brought some freedoms with it, it has also brought fragmentation and new forms of constraint. In particular, by categorizing us according to our preferences, we have become just as straitjacketed as the culture the sex-liberalization movement was trying to correct. This seems counter-intuitive at first glance, but we will see how it works as we go through the chapter. In an area of life where so much is about the prominence of the image, our aim in this chapter is to reframe our approach to sex. We will see how looking at the relationship between sex and technology with new gospel eyes makes all the difference.

For those who are bewildered by the dizzying rate of change, we hope this chapter will bring some perspective. For those going along with the status quo, we hope it will bring a fresh and challenging point of view. For those feeling trapped by a habit or desire, we hope it will point to a path of release. Wherever you are coming from, we believe that only the gracious but true look of Jesus Christ can bring the freedom we crave.

A story of freedom?

In chapter 2, we talked about the modern assumption of progress. The modern story of sex is tightly linked to the story of progress. One of its chief narrators was Michel Foucault. It has often been quipped that the Victorians talked freely about death and repressed sex, whereas now we talk freely about sex and repress death! There is something in this. Foucault's concern was to free sex from the shackles of conservativism:

> The question I would like to pose is not, 'Why are we repressed?' but rather, 'Why do we say, with so much passion and so much resentment . . . that we are repressed? By what spiral did we come to affirm that sex is negated? What led us to show, ostentatiously, that sex is something we hide, to say it is something we silence?'[2]

Foucault was exposing the idea that sex is something 'dirty' or 'shameful', a taboo not to be talked about. 'Where did we get that idea from?' he asks, and 'What makes us think it is right?'

What is remarkable is the way that Foucault's concern to liberalize sex found, in the Internet, the perfect forum. And so almost from its inception sex has occupied a huge proportion of the Internet: its sites, its branding, its functionality. Some commentators claim that over half of all Internet spending is related to sex and at least 20% of Internet users have engaged in the virtual sex described above.[3,4] Whatever the precise figures, no-one doubts the huge place sex has in the digital world.

However, even though sex is such a huge part of the Internet, it is strangely avoided in books about digital technology. *The New Digital Age* is a best-seller vividly painting Google's view of the future, mentioning almost everything else about life online, but it gives just two lines to sex in a 300-page book![5] Many of the other books we have read on the digital age are the same. We have just had a quick look in the index of five prominent ones (Christian and secular) . . . nothing. Why the repression? Sex is clearly a huge part of the online world so why aren't more people talking about it?

The openness of the Bible in talking about sex is often a surprise to people. There are certainly actions, desires and thoughts we will need to say 'no' to. But 'no' is not God's final word. God isn't opposed to sex. The Bible talks freely about sex and sexuality in a way that is honest but never crude, romantic but never unrealistic, dignified without getting it out of proportion.

There is a full book of the Bible devoted to the subject of romance and sexual expression, Song of Solomon. Elsewhere, there are commands to have sex (1 Corinthians 7:5), and exhortations to delight in the diverse joys of sex (Proverbs 5:19).

Perhaps most significantly, the Bible teaches that the joy and intimacy of sex is a God-ordained window on a relationship with him. Just think of that: God dares to say that if you want to know something of what the intimacy and joy of knowing him is like, it is in some way like the closeness and vulnerability of sexual intimacy. Whatever else God will say on this subject, he is not sexually constrained. How could he be – he invented sex!

Talking openly and without crudeness about sex is vital in breaking damaging taboos. A striking example of this has been campaigns against female genital mutilation (FGM). This is not just an African problem: in Europe the number of women threatened by FGM amounts to 500,000, and 4,000 women were treated in London for FGM between 2009 and 2014. Websites, Twitter campaigns, blogs and online appeals have all been instrumental in raising awareness and reaching women in often closed communities to combat this evil. Yet the sexual liberalization story also needs to be challenged. It does not just narrate liberation from the shackles of yesteryear. It assumes ongoing progress in sexuality (the 'P' word crops up again). Consequently, to disagree with culture's view of sexuality is to stand in the way of progress.

So the usual critique of the Bible's view of gender or sex is as Prime Minister David Cameron admonished the Church of England on its debate about women bishops: 'Get with the programme!' Whatever the rights and wrongs of that particular case, the critique is historically short-sighted. First, our culture is nowhere near as 'liberal' as ancient Greco-Roman attitudes, where forms of paedophilia between men and pubescent boys were culturally acceptable and temple prostitution was part of normal day-to-day life. History, in this sense, is more prone to repeat itself than to progress.

Second, part of the appeal of the early church was not that it baptized these views, but that it was able to challenge them. So today, the 'yes' and 'no' of the gospel's challenge is also its appeal. It challenges the claims of liberalization inherent in the culture's story and it appeals to us by showing the unique freedom that comes through living as God intended.

From freedom to fragmentation

Woody Allen quipped, 'Love is the answer, but while you are waiting for the answer, sex raises some pretty good questions!' Mildly amusing as this is, it implies we can separate sex and love. 'Of course we can,' you may think. 'It's just sex. You can't think that all sex involves love.' That all depends on how you understand sex. The view that 'It's just sex!' is so common today that we don't even question it. What we mean with this phrase is that the bodily action of sex can be separated from the emotion and commitment we may or may not choose to attach to it. But what if this is dividing two things that can't be split up? What if this attempt at fragmentation is based on a misunderstanding, even a lie? In the digital age we like to think that we separate things out into neat categories, for example, emotion from intellect, and body from mind. But does life really work like this?

Numerous films and science fiction scenarios reinforce this view. Someone swaps bodies with another person for a period of time (often with comical consequences), all giving force to the idea that 'my body is not me'. But perhaps this is no laughing matter, as Brian Brock comments: 'There is a growing awareness among contemporary philosophers and social theorists of the cultural forces at work offering up a diverse range of variations on the idea that my body is not me.'[6]

The fragmentation doesn't end here. If we can divide a person from his or her body, then we can divide a body up into parts as well. John Wyatt helpfully calls this the 'lego-kit' view of humanity and he critiques it in his excellent book, *Matters of Life and Death*.[7] The Internet and technological advancements in cosmetic surgery give us the tools to do just this. Alongside magazines asking who has the 'best bum of 2014', there are numerous new cosmetic enhancements to help you get onto their list. Surgical procedures originally intended to provide restoration of form and function for those struck by trauma or disease have become big business for those who want to augment a particular body part (note the term).

Why not pause for a moment and reflect. How much of this way of thinking do you unconsciously buy into? Are you tempted to look at a member of the opposite sex in a way that breaks him or her up into constituent parts? How does this impact the way you look at your own body?

Fragmentation can be propagated by the Internet because of the way the virtual world can separate people from context. A pornographic picture of a woman is never set in the context of who she is really: her family background, whether she has any children, or why she has ended up working in the sex industry. Such context would shatter the thin veneer of fantasy around it. We want to focus on just the image, or the body part that arouses us. Anything else merely detracts from the sexual high.

But with all this fragmentation we are noticing the cracks. It is tragically ironic: on the one hand, we are told, 'the body is not you'; on the other, separating the body from what constitutes a person has put a much brighter spotlight on physical appearance.

Articles and images abound, each offering us the 'perfect body' or 'five weeks to rock-hard abs'. With each article we read and image we see, we feel a creeping pressure to match up to the ideals. But the ideals are often airbrushed and unattainable. So the pressure mounts.

In this climate it's painful but not surprising that eating disorders are on the rise; 1.6 million people were suffering from these in the UK in 2014, of which increasing numbers (currently 11%) are male.[8] Body dysmorphic disorder (BDD) – dissatisfaction with your own body – is on the rise too.

It is not just the pressure to have the right body, or body part, but the increasing sexualization of our society. Often we notice the problem most acutely when it affects our children, whether it is the age of first sexual encounter (31% of adolescent men and 29% of adolescent women have their first sexual encounter under the age of sixteen)[9] or a scandal hitting the headlines, such as the case of a teenager who committed suicide because a boy shared her sexting photo around his classmates.[10]

These stories are alarming, not just alarmist. They represent a real issue.

Martin Daubney, the ex-editor of *Loaded*, a popular lads' mag (a men's magazine with mildly pornographic pictures), had debated in defence of the lads' mag culture at Durham University and the Oxford Union. He won by 'quoting carefully selected global government reports and PhD papers that "proved" porn wasn't harmful'.[11] All this changed when he became a father:

> I started seeing the women in my magazine not as sexual objects but as somebody's daughter . . . To think that girls who posed for our magazines had once had their nappies changed, had once been taught to take their first steps and had once been full of childlike hope . . . it was almost heartbreaking.[12]

His honesty is commendable. Arguably less commendable is the way the *Daily Mail*, which published this article online, presented it alongside an advertising sidebar with soft-porn images to click on. But that's precisely the issue; fragmentation is so prevalent that we can even fragment our disapproval from our user habits.

Our scope in this chapter is not to provide a pastoral framework to deal with pornography, eating disorders or BDD. There are other books with that aim that do it well.[13] Instead we want to identify the broader trends that underpin the changing perceptions of sex and sexuality in our digital age. We want to show that our freedom is being undermined by fragmentation.

Free to choose?

Part of the drive behind this fragmentation has been a desire to break down the traditional categories used to define us. Media researcher Johanna Blakley has given an impassioned call for an end to the traditional demographics of 'Old Media' that straitjackets people by categorizing them according to such things as race, gender and age.[14] Instead social media has allowed us to determine the communities we want to be part of, and we self-define on the basis of preference. These new 'taste communities' capture our likes and, she argues, are a much truer representation of who we really are.

Certainly preference is important and, as we dealt with in chapter 4 on identity, the traditional categories of defining people can be constraining. None of us like the idea of being pigeonholed according to gender, class, ethnicity or age. All of us want to be treated as people and not categories.

The question that we need to explore is whether self-defining by preference is any better. Does it really deliver the freedom it offers?

When Blakley crescendoed in her nine-minute TED talk with the line, 'I would much rather know that you like *Buffy the Vampire Slayer* than how old you are', we found ourselves thinking, 'Really?' Does either detail alone tell us all that much about a person? Then, perhaps more suspiciously, we thought, 'Of course you want to know what our preferences are! Then you can sell us something!' We know, we're terrible cynics.

But this raises the question: if we define ourselves by our preferences, who or what is really in the driving seat?

What has all this to do with sexuality? Sexuality is a key area where there is a strong drive to define people by preferences. In 2014 Facebook released a new feature that enabled users to choose from one of seventy-one gender options, including intersex, non-binary, agender, gender fluid, trans, trans female, trans male, trans person, trans woman . . . and so on. It's a long list.

Facebook worked with UK group Press for Change in coming up with the list. 'Gender identities are complex and, for many people, describing themselves as just a man or woman has always been inadequate,' said Stephen Whittle, vice-president of Press for Change.[15]

We should not think that technology is neutral in this. It is pivotal. First, technology is allowing new terms to be developed because the technology exists to modify the human body like never before. As the technology has developed, 'transsexual' and 'sex-reassignment surgery' have become part of common language. As these terms are used more and more, they in turn influence how we see ourselves and those around us. Gender categories that were once seen as fixed and unchangeable are now seen as fluid and interchangeable.

Second, the re-categorization of life along 'preference' lines is shaped by the structure at the core of the virtual world. The network of the Web was set up this way from the off. It is part of its 'distributed' structure that we commented on in chapter 5, where people self-select their networks and connections. It is not so much that we have decided to orientate life around preferences because that is how life works best. Instead the structure inherent in technology, and set up by a select few at the heart of the Web revolution, is redefining our identities along preference lines.

This 'preference orientation' is being worked out in gender definitions as outlined above. It is also being worked out in the proliferation and commoditization of sex.

'What's the problem with that?' you may be thinking. 'Aren't these now more fluid categories, giving us greater freedom?' The problem is that it is naive to think that as users we are solely in control of what we choose. We may click the link and select the category, but this vastly underestimates how well honed the marketing machines and media have become at shaping our preferences. All the personalized browser experiences and user-specific adverts are not just offering us what we want but shaping what we want.

A study in the US *Journal of Adolescent Health* of over 1,000 teenagers concluded that the 'strong relationship between media and adolescents' sexual expression may be due to the media's role as an important source of sexual socialization for teenagers'.[16] 'Media' in this study was a very broad category including films, TV, music, magazines and, of course, the adverts included in all of these. In other words, media and marketing shapes adolescent preferences.

That leads to some uncomfortable questions. If we express our freedom through our preferences, but our preferences themselves are shaped in large part by the structure of the Web and media, then are our preferences really free? In fact, am I free? Could it be that my desires have been significantly moulded by the well-honed marketing machines of big business? Could I be more a creature of my culture than I realize or want to admit?

A colleague at church runs an anti-addiction course. Increasingly both men and women come onto the course for addiction to pornography. One of the great problems he and his wife help them to realize is that pornography has changed their perception of sex and their sexual partner. In fact pornography has not just changed their perception but changed the neurological pathways that cause the pleasure sensation associated with arousal and orgasm – a discovery that has been widely documented in journals and publications of the past few years. This has two effects to which he alerts them. First, they will crave more novel pornographic content (usually harder pornography) for the same high. Second, their ability to experience pleasure with a partner will be greatly diminished because of the impact of pornography on their brain. The effects are not necessarily permanent but they are very embedded and require long-term persistence fuelled by God's grace to reverse.

Something that promised freedom has actually enslaved people.

The look of liberty

Throughout this book, we have seen that technology is not just the tools we make but a way of looking at the world. We have used two main illustrations for this: the story that technology tells and the technological frame we look through.[17] This idea of looking is so important to sexuality in the digital age. How do I perceive others, how do I see myself, how do I look at the world around me?

Imagine a party where halfway through the evening, people realize that one of the female guests is a prostitute. Think of all the different ways people may look at her. One looks down his nose with disgust; another looks lustfully, hoping to end the night with her; another looks at her as an object of pity; another doesn't give her another thought and carries on enjoying the party.

Then think about how she may see herself. Does she see herself as a victim enslaved by others, as empowered by her ability to entice men? Perhaps she sees herself as a source of shame to her family. Perhaps none of these – she's just enjoying the party? What is the true perspective?

One of the remarkable things about Jesus is how he looks at people. His look is always life-giving. In the Gospels we see this in how people respond to him. The outcasts flock to him. Would they do that if he looked with dismissive condemnation? Those who've made a mess of life are drawn to him but then see themselves both as affirmed and challenged. The self-righteous find his look uncomfortable, the proud humbling, the lowly uplifting.

It is not just how he looks at people; it is how his look changes them. It changes how they see themselves and how they see others. That is why the Gospel writers use Jesus' healings of blind people as illustrations of spiritual sight.[18] Jesus teaches, 'The eye is the lamp of the body. So, if your eye is healthy, your whole body will be full of light, but if your eye is bad, your whole body will be full of darkness' (Matthew 6:22–23). He is saying that perception is much more important than just a way of looking at the world; it affects us – every part of us, including our bodies!

It was telling how the ex-editor of *Loaded*, Martin Daubney, narrated his turning point: 'I started seeing the women in my magazine not as sexual objects but as somebody's daughter.' He looked at them differently.

We have a friend who, when he worked in the city, battled against lust on his daily commute by praying for those he was tempted to objectify. It was a wonderful response because it changed how he looked at them – as people before God, not objects to be desired.

Perception is not purely subjective, just a matter of how we choose to see the world. There are right and wrong ways of seeing. Equally there are things we should not look at. The psalmist's resolution, 'I will not set before my eyes anything that is worthless' (Psalm 101:3), is important. There is lots of good 'accountability software' that can help in this area, and many broadband providers have parental control options – often a control that is just as helpful for adults. We often hear people say, 'I don't have an issue so I don't need one of those', but when they are so cheap and easy to use, is not prevention better than cure, especially when pornographic content producers are so aggressive and practised at getting people hooked?

The challenge we are highlighting is to see the world as it really is. But how can we do that when our perception is so influenced by other factors: nature, nurture, culture and the frame of technology? Jesus teaches, 'Truly, truly, I say to you, unless one is born again he cannot see the kingdom of God' (John 3:3). This new start happens as we come to Jesus and the Spirit renews us. Think of how God looks at us. 'Man looks on the outward appearance but the LORD looks on the heart' (1 Samuel 16:7).

Some of us think this verse is comforting – 'even if on the outside we don't feel up to much, at least God sees what we are really like.' But really it is very challenging. Have you looked at your heart and seen it as it really is? All of our hearts are distorted sexually and fragmented.

The cross shows what God truly sees when he looks at the heart. We are so sinful that Jesus Christ had to die on the cross for us. There was no other way. But Jesus' look is also restoring. He did not come to condemn us but to bring us life. The cross shows us that we are so loved by Jesus Christ that he was prepared to die for us. Challenged and loved, laid low and lifted up, denied and affirmed.

> Forever etched upon my mind
> Is the look of him who died
> The Lamb I crucified
> And now my life will sing the praise
> Of pure atoning grace
> That looked on me and gladly took my place.[19]

This is how Jesus looks at us, and it radically shifts how we see the world.

Pornography is built on a perception trick. It looks like it is about freedom, empowerment and relationship. It loses its hold on us when we see it as it really is: enslaving, demeaning and commoditizing sex.

Similarly, the cosmetic and fitness industries are all about perception. They entice us to see ourselves as our bodies, and our bodies as parts that can be augmented and improved.

What if we resisted at the first premise? If our digital age has caused fragmentation and a gradual pulling apart of the whole, then freedom is found in putting the picture back together. Freedom has been sold to us as 'be whatever you want to be and do whatever you want to do' – your preferences are what define you. But freedom is only doing what we choose when our desires are rightly ordered. This is why seeing the world through the eyes of Scripture is so important. In a world where different opinions abound, it gives us God's perspective on whatever is true, whatever is honourable, whatever is just, whatever is pure, whatever is lovely, whatever is commendable (Philippians 4:8).

What if we saw ourselves as whole people, a glorious integration of our bodies, our personalities, our spiritualities? Even the cosmetic industry knows this fragmentation can't be right, which is why ironically you will have seen endless beauty adverts about 'wholeness' and 'well-being'.

Facebook may feel it is giving us more choice with its seventy-one different options for sexuality, but what it is actually doing is eroding the true view of reality: 'So God created man in his own image, in the image of God he created him; male and female he created them' (Genesis 1:27). Far from being constraining, if this is the way that God has made us, then seeing ourselves as one of two genders, and gender not as a part that can be changed but as an integrated whole, is the liberating true perspective.

Ephesians 2:10 tells us, 'For we are his workmanship, created in Christ Jesus for good works'. Think of the Monet masterpiece *Les Nymphéas*. If you haven't seen it then do look it up. Ask yourself, 'What happens if I were to remove the colour blue from the picture, or if I were to take out the water lilies, or if I were to change the greens for reds?' The painting doesn't just lose a part; the whole is changed. It ceases to be the masterpiece it once was. In fact, because we know it is a masterpiece, no-one would dream of trying to pull it apart like this.

Hopefully you get the point. We are God's masterpiece, created as a whole with unimaginable glory and beauty. Yes, the masterpiece has been spoiled by sin, but the look of the Master Craftsman restores us, and one day soon the masterpiece will again be complete.

Questions

1. What are the particular stories of freedom that you are tempted to believe in the area of sexuality? (Think of the narratives we have explored: the sexual liberalization story that we're getting more progressive; the fragmentation story that you are a sum of your body parts; the choice/freedom story that real liberty is found in exercising your choice, not primarily in being the person God wants you to be.)
2. Reflect on those stories and how they promise life and freedom. What is the reality?
3. What are the ways that you are tempted to fragment others or yourself? How do you see this in the area of sexual images on the Internet and TV, or in magazines?

How do you see this in other areas such as your own attractiveness?

4. What are some of the key words that come into your mind when asked, 'How would you describe yourself?' Given the answer to this question, in what ways are you tempted to define yourself by your preferences?

5. Think of what influences you in your perception of gender and sexuality. What websites, books, cultural opinions, TV programmes and/or magazines are important to you? How are your preferences open to change and manipulation?

6. How might the way Jesus sees you challenge and affirm you and lead to change?

7. What one thing are you going to change as a result of reading this chapter? (Something you need to stop looking at, some way of looking at others/yourself you need to change, a truth about Jesus' look that you need to remember and pray through?)

Searching for knowledge

In October 2012, *The Times* carried an article called 'Google, the next generation, will be beaming up everywhere'.[1] In it Amit Singhal, vice-president of Google, was reported as saying that the company is near to creating a kind of *Star Trek* device that constantly surrounds us, ready to supply answers to our various questions. Google was proposing that a voice-activated, constantly-with-us search-engine assistant could provide near-instant access to knowledge! Apple was already on the task. The early versions of the iPhone voice assistant Siri may have been a bit glitchy, but it wasn't long before the voice-activated search engine was a reality. Android phones have got their own versions: Skyvi, Iris, Robin, Vlingo, Maluuba; and Microsoft has Cortana (to mention just a few).

The names may be a little odd but the concept is compelling. Want to recognize a song? Looking for a restaurant or bar near you? Can't remember something or perhaps you never knew it in the first place? Voice-activate the search engine and now you 'know' it. When the information is right there, what difference does it make whether that information is in your brain or in a server?

Of course the speed of access to a vast sea of information has had much more profound implications than just settling pub debates about trivia, or identifying a catchy tune.

Think of the huge role that the Internet and social media played in the Arab Spring. Information about what was happening in other states was quickly disseminated through the Internet – through official 24/7 news channels, but more strikingly through the personal testimonies of texts, tweets, Facebook updates and blogs. There were extensive informal social networks generating an increasing momentum for change. The very word 'revolution' became as much an Internet theme as a street-based rally cry. Tweets containing the word exploded from 2,300 per day to more than 230,000 per day.[2]

The speed and breadth of information available leads some to talk about 'democratized' knowledge, where knowledge is available to the many and no longer just the preserve of the academic elite.

Certainly there is more information 'out there' for users to access. With a sufficiently quick Internet connection and a click of a button, anyone in a few moments can be listening to a business lecture from Harvard. The Internet has extended our reach and access to new information that otherwise we might not have known. That fosters greater innovation and creativity. It's hard to argue with claims that this has significantly enriched our lives. We have much to be thankful for in our search-engine age.

But equally there are challenges. There may be more information 'out there', but who is controlling it? We like to think of the Internet as a free environment, but big businesses and states are getting very adept at controlling the data flow. For many the Internet was seen as a tool that would usher in an age where such ubiquitous access to data would make it impossible for secrets to be kept (at least for long). Armed with the truth, humanity would be unhindered in its march of progress.

But such ideals need to be set against the hard reality of spin doctors, marketing, and the realization that more information often means more data to sift through as we try to discern what and whom we can trust.

This chapter will explore knowledge in our digital age and particularly the claims that we suffer from information excess. We'll suggest that while there is more data for us to process, our problem is not so much the information itself but the way it exposes cracks in our view of knowledge. By reintegrating knowledge with wisdom, we'll rediscover God's place in our pursuit and use of knowledge. As we do this we'll see the joy of an integrated view of knowledge that enables us to thrive and flourish as we use what we know to glorify God and love others.

Coping with data smog

As we have more information, an important question to ask is: has this translated into us living better? In some sense the proliferation of information has created a kind of 'data smog' where we struggle to see our way through all the messages that crowd around us.

A team at the University of Southern California calculated that in the West, the average person is bombarded by the equivalent of 174 newspapers of data every day.[3] Even if we feel this number is overestimated, few would doubt that we are in the midst of an information glut. Our challenge is how we filter through all this information to find what is true, important and meaningful.

A while back an AOL employee leaked the search log data of more than 650,000 of its users, and commentators jumped on the opportunity to analyse normally private information. Particularly poignant was how many use their search window as a kind of personal therapist. User 3696023's searches were not unusual: 'I hurt when I think too much', 'I love road trips', 'I hate my weight' and 'I fear being alone for the rest of my life'. One journalist commented, 'Me too, 3696023. Me too.'[4]

All of us know the caricature of the academic who, though very knowledgeable, cannot tie his own shoelaces. With headlines in the West about family breakdown, increasing rates of depression and rampant consumerism, is there a danger that as a culture we are becoming more like the caricature: increasingly knowledgeable, but unable to cope with life?

Equally, as the amount of information grows, we seem to have a tendency to latch on to the 'pithy' or sensational rather than the significant.

Early in the life of Twitter, BBC Radio 4 hosted a programme discussing how it was changing politics. Previously that year the UK Chancellor's budget had been hijacked by '#Pasty tax'. It is a great hashtag – instantly memorable and mildly amusing – but all of the commentators agreed that the government's update of the tax regulations regarding certain baked goods was not even close to being a central part of the budget. It was a mundane bit of bureaucracy, bringing tax on hot food into line with all other products. The opposition political parties had not noticed it buried in the minutiae of the budget nor did they think it was an issue worth mentioning. In real terms its impact on people was negligible, but it was a great slogan and so it dominated the discussion of the budget for two weeks. It trumped the important issues like reducing the budget deficit and unemployment.

As the availability of information broadens the social conversation, surely we must ask whether that conversation is improving as a result.

Life is not a game of Trivial Pursuit

The search engine is a phenomenal tool, but mere access to knowledge does not necessarily make us better able to live in the world. Why would it? Life is not a game of Trivial Pursuit. As T. S. Eliot warned in his poem 'The Rock',

> Where is the Life we have lost in living?
> Where is the wisdom we have lost in knowledge?
> Where is the knowledge we have lost in information?[5]

Today many focus on the quantity of information as our main problem. Commentators talk a lot about 'drowning' or 'sinking' in data, but perhaps this glut of information is not the primary problem. Perhaps it just accentuates the problem. If you have a crack in the roof of your house, you notice it much more quickly when it rains hard than when it drizzles. The rain is not the real problem. The crack is the problem.

What if our problem is not so much the information overload but the cracks it is exposing? What if we have let cracks form by knowledge becoming disconnected from real life, and access to information becoming disconnected from our capacity to think and put it into action? If this is an accurate assessment, then focusing on the deluge is missing the real issue. Fix the cracks and it can pour and pour but the house will remain waterproof.

Repairing the cracks: the search engine is not enough

A large crack that we have today is that we talk a lot about knowledge but very little about wisdom. In the ancient world 'wisdom' was a dominant theme in literature, but today it seems to have been reduced to a few pithy quotes in the 'wit and wisdom' pages of magazines.

If you read the newspapers, people have a lot to say about ethics (right and wrong) and knowledge. But when we pause to think of our lives, the vast majority of our daily living does not fit neatly into either of these categories.

How do I respond to a difficult person in a conversation? How do I cope with stress at work? Should I spend more money to get free-range meat or save money and give it to a homeless charity? How do I improve my relationship with my teenage daughter? Should I buy these trousers when I don't need them but I do like them? How do I help my friend when he needs help but says he doesn't want help?

These questions are the stuff of life. They aren't less than ethics, but they are not ethical decisions alone. While they are informed by knowledge, knowledge by itself is not enough to answer them. They require wisdom.

The search engine is not enough.

In the Bible, knowledge is always bound up with how we live. What we know influences and changes how we act.

In particular, the Bible has a lot to say about wisdom. In Proverbs 4:7 we are told that 'The beginning of wisdom is this: Get wisdom'! Part of the reason that the Bible places such a high value on wisdom is that it is a guiding principle woven into the fabric of the world:

When he established the heavens, I [wisdom] was there . . .
when he assigned the sea to its limit,

so that the waters might not transgress his command,
when he marked out the foundations of the earth,
    then I was beside him, like a master workman . . .
(Proverbs 8:27–30)

What this means is that just as there are physical laws in the universe, so there are moral laws expressing wisdom in the universe. Consequently, just as if I neglect the laws of mass and density when making a boat I will sink, so if I neglect the laws of wisdom then I may find myself sinking in life. I wonder, as you reflect, what are the areas where you feel you are sinking for lack of wisdom?

The Christian thinker Augustine of Hippo (354–430), writing at the turn of the fifth century AD, distinguished between *sapientia* (wisdom) and *scientia* (knowledge).[6] Crucially for Augustine, knowledge is connected to wisdom, but it is subordinate. It is to inform it, but it is its servant.

This means that knowledge must always be seen in a practical context; any issue of knowledge must always be connected to and put in the context of wisdom. Wisdom is the great 'so what' of life. 'So you know a lot of things, but how is that knowledge translating to better living?'

We can see the problems of not asking this question all around us today. We spend billions of pounds pursuing knowledge and technological advancement, but in contrast hardly anything on how to live well. We know more about our world and universe than any other generation and have amazing power to effect change in the world, but seem unable to know what to do with that power. We understand ourselves biologically better than ever before, but do not seem able to understand how to be content and fulfilled.

What we need is to put knowledge back into the context of wisdom.

What if we were less interested in the sensationalism of a celebrity culture, where the supreme virtue seems to be to know the latest bit of gossip, and more interested in what would develop us as people and help us better to engage in the world? What if we assigned less importance to the letters before or after a person's name (Prof./PhD) and more importance to how he or she lives?

How about pausing when you are next about to type into the search engine (or at least reflecting on your search engine history) and asking yourself: why am I searching for this? Really? Is knowing this going to enrich my life and help me to live better? Starting to question in this way is a key step to help us think about seeing knowledge and wisdom in a much more integrated way. In our experience there is no quick fix. Instead it requires a process of retraining how we think – to help us think wisely. But as we start to reconnect knowledge and wisdom we will begin to fill in one of the big cracks in our search-engine age.

Repairing the cracks: seeing the wider picture

Back in 2006, a piece of research had big implications for the legal and justice system, particularly in the United States. Prior to the study, law courts (and the public at large) had assumed that fingerprint analysis was a simple matter of true or false. 'Matching' a fingerprint to a crime scene was often a crucial turning point in getting a conviction; after all, it is either a match or not, right?

Apparently not. The study cast doubt on this assumption. It demonstrated that the mental state of those conducting the fingerprint analysis had a significant impact on results.[7] Crudely put, the test was not neutral. If the person conducting the test thought there was a likelihood that it would give a positive result then the test would be affected by that bias and a positive outcome was significantly more likely, and vice versa.

This led to many convictions being overturned and a much greater rigour about the impartiality of those conducting the forensic test. The study commented,

> The human mind is not a camera and we do not passively process information. We engage in a variety of active [mental] processes that organise and impose structure on the information as it comes in from the external world . . . we effect [sic] what we see, how we interpret it and evaluate it, and our decision making processes.[8]

Our culture is very aware of reader bias in arts disciplines like literature and philosophy, but curiously naive when it comes to science. The shock of the study is how it implies that in any area of knowledge, even something as binary as a true/false fingerprint analysis, our overall outlook significantly influences what we think we know.

The book of Proverbs has a lot to say about the right outlook on life. It makes the bold statements first that 'the fear of the LORD is the beginning of knowledge' (1:7) and second that 'the fear of the LORD is the beginning of wisdom' (9:10). Why is this? Doesn't it sound odd (to say the least) to claim that to really begin to know anything or be wise about anything, you need to fear God?

What it is saying is that holding God in reverence and awe (fear) is foundational to rightly interpreting, evaluating and interacting with the world around us. There are two essential truths to build our lives on:

1. There is a God at the centre of the universe.
2. He is to be held in reverence and awe.

Unless we have these baseline convictions in place, we will, to put it mildly, always have major cracks in our lives.

One of the reasons we find this so difficult to accept is because of the common assumption that we are impartial processors of information. The research mentioned above is just one striking piece in a rapidly growing area of neuropsychology. It is helping us to grasp what the Bible tells us plainly about how much we influence what we perceive to be 'true' or 'reliable'.

We are not mere logical calculators that accept truth and reject falsehood. We are dynamic processors, and our predispositions, expectations and assumptions significantly colour what we think we know. This is not to say that our assumptions can't be corrected by new information, but it is to say that we are nowhere near as impartial as we like to think.

The great Anglican theologian Thomas Cranmer drew from the Bible the insight that can be summarized as, 'What the heart loves, the will chooses and the intellect justifies.'[9] If you doubt this, just think of a time when you had to persuade someone that a relationship they were in was bad for them. It is very hard to get such a person to 'see' what to everyone else is obvious, whatever the evidence. Our hearts shape what we think we know.

Why does this matter? Well, if our baseline assumptions about the world we live in have a big impact on what we think we know and how we live, then we have to reflect on these assumptions.

For example, a powerful system of belief in the West over the past generation has been the ideology of materialism, which argues that the material world is all there is and all that matters. One of the core assumptions of this philosophy is that we should only trust what we can investigate 'scientifically' (though ironically we can't scientifically investigate this core assumption itself!).

Such a system of belief tells us that the world has come about purely as a result of random cosmic forces and that it has no ultimate meaning or purpose. Is it any wonder then that as this worldview has grown in popularity, our culture has been marked by an increasing focus on and desire for the material (hence increasing consumerism) and a loss of hope in the future (hence increasing short-termism)? What we believe impacts what we think we know and therefore how we live.

In contrast we need to remember the truth of God's story of life that we outlined in chapter 2. In a world that is often orientated around the accumulation of things, we need to reflect on God's place at the centre of the story and the need to orientate our lives in all things around God. To pick up on a previous metaphor, this is the reality ingrained throughout the world. It is the meaning of life! (It only took us to chapter 8 to tell you!)

Consequently it is also the purpose for which God gives us knowledge: so that we can give him glory as we flourish in relationship with him.

Whatever other baseline convictions we have about the world, if they are not in line with this biblical perspective, then we will always be cutting against the grain of the world. We will also be deeply offending the generous God who has given us the life we enjoy. We may make observations about the world, but we will never fit them into the overarching purpose that really makes sense of them. We will be able to do some meaningful actions in the world, but those actions will always miss the greater purpose, why we are here.

That is why Proverbs tells us that fear of the Lord is the beginning of knowledge and wisdom. It is not an archaic idea.

It is a fiercely contemporary reminder that without a baseline belief in the God of the Bible, our knowledge and lives will always be seriously flawed.

In contrast, though, there's a beautiful harmony of knowledge and action when the wider purpose is embraced. This is why the Bible is such an 'envisioning' document. Time and time again it sets before us the ideal of what life can (and should) look like as we live to glorify God, loving him, loving one another under him and properly caring for his world.

Supremely, this vision is embodied in the perfect life and teaching of the Lord Jesus Christ. Through him, the Bible is saying to us, 'This is how life should be lived: isn't there a beauty about such a life? Don't you want to live this way?' Little wonder that Jesus has been called the 'luminous Nazarene' for the way he lights up history.

Integrating knowledge back into life

Think of how this integrated view of knowledge applies in the two great areas of life: love for God and love for neighbour (Matthew 22:36–40).

One of the transforming insights the ancient thinker Augustine gives us is that all knowledge and wisdom is devotional – it is to be used to help us love God more. Romans 1:20 talks of creation revealing God's character and nature to us. A few weeks ago a Christian friend sent me (Pete) a link to a video about how a pufferfish attracts its mate. It sounded a bit silly, but I watched it.

The pufferfish makes a pattern in the sand of such incredible intricacy and beauty that I was left genuinely speechless. Search 'Pufferfish sand pattern' if you have a moment to see it; it is astonishing. What should I do with such information? Say, 'Wow, isn't that a clever fish?' Store the information away so that I can impress someone when there's a lull in conversation? Shrug my shoulders and move on, having had a moment's distraction from a hard day? All of these reactions miss the point. The pufferfish gives us an insight into God's beauty, his creativity, his ingenuity, his sheer playfulness, in short his glory. The video should lead me to praise him and worship him. So it is with all knowledge. It gives us an insight into God's world, which gives us an insight into him, which leads to thanks, praise and worship.

We come across so much information that we cannot process it all and turn it into thanks and praise to God. But why not put this into practice with a few things each day? What new piece of information have you come across today that gives you a window on God's glory? Why not pause to praise and thank him for it?

Second, we need to take care with knowledge that it is used to build others up and not to cut them down. 'Knowledge is power', but what kind of power? Is it a force for good or destructive? Is it there to build people up or build myself up? My father-in-law regularly cuts out sections of the newspaper for my wife and me. Small articles that are of interest or may be helpful. I really appreciate it. It struck me recently that this is a very different use of knowledge from one I tend to fall into: I read something and find myself telling others later in a way that leaves them impressed with my knowledge but, if I'm honest, is more self-serving than neighbour-loving.

Today we have more information coming our way than ever before. In one sense we have the capacity to be more knowledgeable than ever before, but what will we do with this knowledge? If the statistics about search engines are anything to go by, then our supreme concerns seem to be buying things, knowing the latest piece of celebrity gossip, and sex. Is this really the best we can do?

Is it not a much more attractive and meaningful vision to seek to use knowledge to enrich others, to benefit the world around us, and in so doing to glorify supremely the generous God who gives us knowledge in the first place?

If the first step we outlined above in addressing the cracks in the roof is to rediscover a concern for wisdom and living life well, then the second step is to recognize that wisdom comes by putting God back at the centre of the picture. Only when we start to operate with him as our integration point can we truly make sense of the world we are in and therefore start to see how to live wisely in it.

Questions

1. What does your browser history reveal about what you prioritize and the functional purpose of your life (the direction you are actually heading in rather than the direction you would like to be heading in)?

2. What information feeds do you prioritize in your life? What information feeds could help you to live better in God's world?

   What do you do with the information that you receive? Instead, how could you use it to glorify God, to love him, love others and live better in his world?

3. How could your life look different if you properly used the information you have received today?

Conclusion: Truly human

The year is AD 429 and the East Germanic tribe known to history as the Vandals have surrounded the Roman city of Hippo. Augustine, the bishop of Hippo, lies dying in his bed. He wouldn't live to see the end of Rome that he foresaw, but it came as he anticipated. Twenty-five years after his death the Vandals sacked Rome, and the empire that had ruled for five hundred years and over five million square kilometres lay in ruins. The Roman vision of political stability and universal peace under the rule of the emperor had been forced to give way to a new world order.

In his famous book, *The City of God*, St Augustine responded to those in his day who were arguing that the end of the empire meant the end of the biblical God. As Augustine wrote in the early part of the fifth century, the old order was crumbling around him. He addressed two questions: what future was there for the God who had been taken to be the God of the Roman world? And how should people live in the world in such a time of transition?

Many people have made parallels between Augustine's day and our own. Through the advances of science and technology, the modern world seems to be coming into its own and the structures of the old world are creaking. The question we might well ask is similar to that of the Roman sceptics: does the new digital world have any room for the old order's God? Through this book we have been arguing that the place of God in the digital world is the same place he has always occupied. It is the nature of human kingdoms to come and go, but not so for God's rule. Some find the present time of change unsettling; for others it is exciting. And for those born more recently, it's just the way things are, the world they have always known. Whichever group you are in, you don't have to read much history to know that many such times of change have existed in the past. A consequence of our limited lifespan has always led people to emphasize the events and concerns of their own day and play down the transitions of previous centuries. The digital world hasn't left God fighting for his life. How could it? His love, and his kingdom, endures forever.

Augustine responded to the sceptics by contrasting life in two different cities: the City of Man and the City of God. The City of Man is the world human beings have made. It holds within it much that is good, but it has no room for God. In this city people own life as their possession and seek the power to extend their own authority and control. By contrast, the City of God has a heavenly Master Builder. He gives life in this city to people as a gift. Life is to be received with open hands and lived with whole hearts in service of others and to bring glory to him. God builds this city, but he uses human work so that we can know the privilege of life as co-labourers and enjoy the satisfaction of a job well done. The City of Man, Augustine argued, was the city that was passing away. The City of God, by contrast, could never be overthrown.

The immediate crisis in the Roman Empire was part of a much larger story that was the history of conflict between the two cities. This narrative does not belong to any one age or empire but is the narrative of all of human history, the narrative within which human empires continue to rise and fall. It is the same story within which we are still living today.

Tech City

In which of Augustine's two cities do you think technology belongs? It is a hard question. How about we make it more specific? In which city do cars belong? Or computers? That doesn't seem to make it any easier.

The answer, of course, is both. And that is why the questions of technology that we have been considering in this book are complicated questions. That is why this book is shaped by an approach that seeks to hold together both the 'yes' and 'no' to technology. As we explored in chapter 3, the two must always come together.

In the end the simplistic answers – the ones that give either a digital 0 or 1 to technology – break down. A robust approach requires careful thinking about the story that technology operates within. It requires reflection on our use. It requires conversation with others. It requires effort in practices that we can't just take off the shelf but must seek to embed into the pattern of our lives.

And, of course, it doesn't end with this book. We are well aware in our own lives how our engagement with the issues we have been discussing is really only just beginning. In the years ahead the specific technologies, gadgets and apps will change. Some of the issues will take on different aspects, and new issues will come to the fore. But the underlying conflict of history's two cities will continue to make the deepest questions the age-old ones. The particular configuration of the issues might be new, and the historic landscape might have changed, but the underlying story remains the same one. As Martin Heidegger put it, 'The essence of technology is by no means anything technological.'[1]

Tech life

This book is based on two foundational points about technology. The first one is the one we have just described, that technology's essence is not really technological. This is an important point to grasp if you aren't particularly technologically minded. The place of technology in our world and in our lives isn't something we can leave to the programmers and pioneers.

It is also an essential point to grasp if tech is your thing. It can be easy to dismiss as disengaged those who are a little bit slower on the uptake when it comes to new technology, those who prefer to keep their distance from the cutting edge. We all need to be engaged in the conversation about technology, and we need to draw others into discussion with us.

Whenever I (Ed) speak on technology in a church setting, I always make a point of talking afterwards to the elderly people present. These conversations often follow a similar pattern: I thank them for listening and ask for their thoughts on how technology is impacting life in our world. They pause. Then they start to talk about how things used to be in the past. They tell me that they feel alienated from the conversation about technology because it seems to be about a world they no longer feel they know. They encourage me and tell me how pleased they are that I am addressing these issues, but they don't think they have very much to contribute. I seek to respectfully disagree. Older people are just the people to bring into conversations on technology, not because they are the avid users of the latest apps but because the questions of technology are questions of human life. And life is something elderly people tend to know a great deal about.

This is the second key point: the questions that technology raises are the age-old questions of human life. We have seen this throughout the book. Technology has been the constant backdrop, but our journey has taken us through the familiar issues of life. We have considered human identity, community and history. We have discussed time, wisdom and sex. The transforming vision that we have been seeking to hold out is a renewed vision of the ordinary human life. This real life in the digital world is life built on God. Established on him, we become increasingly who he made us to be, able to live rooted lives through the changing tide of culture.

How to live before you die

On 12 June 2005, Steve Jobs stood before the leaving students of Stanford University as the guest speaker at their degree ceremony. Jobs spoke powerfully from his own experience, passing on the lessons he had learnt about how to make the most of life. The title of his talk: 'How to live before you die'.

The founder of Apple, who became the tech guru of a generation, had three lessons he wanted to pass on. The first was about the need to trust that the dots of life will join up, that things will work out: 'You have to trust in something – your gut, destiny, life, karma, whatever.' His second was about work: 'You've got to find what you love,' he told the students. 'Keep looking until you find it. Don't settle.' Then Steve Jobs broke one of the fundamental social taboos. He talked about death. A year earlier he had been diagnosed with the cancer that would kill him at the age of fifty-six. But at the time of the talk it seemed that he had been cured. He spoke, so he said, as one who had faced death and 'lived through it'. We looked at his message in chapter 1, but it is worth quoting again:

> Your time is limited, so don't waste it living someone else's life. Don't be trapped by dogma – which is living with the results of other people's thinking. Don't let the noise of others' opinions drown out your own inner voice. And, most important, have the courage to follow your heart and intuition. They somehow already know what you truly want to become. Everything else is secondary.[2]

This advice from one of the icons of our age gets to the heart of the modern world's vision of life to the full. It is all the more significant because it comes from a man who once dressed up as Jesus Christ for an Apple party and has been heralded as the messiah of the digital world!

Heidi Campbell is an academic who focuses on the field of communications. She has spent a long time researching the Apple phenomenon and in 2010 co-authored a paper outlining the religious significance which Apple products are designed to embody.[3] In an interview marking what would have been Steve Jobs' sixtieth birthday in 2015, Campbell was asked about the way he continues to be revered in society. In Jobs, she argues, 'We have a messianic figure that led people, brought new life to the technology when it was almost dead, and created transformational technology from nothing.'[4]

But as beautiful and satisfying as many Apple products are (I am typing this on a MacBook), this modern messiah and his message are both deeply flawed. Walter Isaacson draws this out in his authorized biography of Jobs, written following long conversations with the man himself and those closest to him.

Reading Isaacson's account, there is no doubt that in Steve Jobs the world knew a man of incredible ability, an almost prophetic figure who seemed to know what the world wanted before the world knew itself. But those who knew Jobs also knew another side to the public persona. He was frequently domineering and disrespectful, often treating those closest to him at Apple and in his personal relationships with disdain. He was his own man, committed to following his heart and intuition in accord with the advice he gave to the students at Stanford. When others didn't fit in with his ideas, that was their problem.

An early example of Jobs' flawed brilliance comes from a programming job he held at Atari (the computer game manufacturer) shortly after he dropped out of college. This is how Isaacson tells the story:

> Alcorn assigned him to work with a straitlaced engineer named Don Lang. The next day Lang complained, 'This guy's a goddamn hippie with b.o. Why did you do this to me? And he's impossible to deal with.' Jobs clung to the belief that his fruit-heavy vegetarian diet would prevent not just mucus but also body odour, even if he didn't use deodorant or shower regularly. It was a flawed theory. Lang and others wanted to let Jobs go, but Bushnell worked out a solution. 'The smell and behaviour wasn't an issue with me,' he said. 'Steve was prickly, but I kind of liked him. So I asked him to go on the night shift. It was a way to save him.' Jobs would come in after Lang and others had left and work through most of the night. Even thus isolated, he became known for his brashness. On those occasions when he happened to interact with others, he was prone to informing them that they were 'dumb s***s'. In retrospect, he stands by that judgment. 'The only reason I shone was that everyone else was so bad,' Jobs recalled.[5]

It is a funny story. But there is a serious edge to it in what it reveals about Jobs' character. We are left to ask whether this is the kind of example that Jobs wanted a generation to follow when he called the Stanford students to 'live before you die'.

Truly human

At Stanford, Jobs acted the part of the man who had lived through death, teaching his disciples on how to live before they died. Perhaps Jobs really did consider himself something of a modern-day messiah. In any case, the Atari story shows the underlying reality: Jobs was the saviour whose feet needed a wash!

The contrast with the true Messiah couldn't be clearer. As Jesus approached his own death, John 13 records how he gathered together his disciples in Jerusalem to teach them how to live in his absence. During supper Jesus got up. He took a towel, poured water into a basin and began to wash the disciples' feet. It is a staggering act of humility. The Son of God doing the work of a servant, using his power and authority to take account of the needs of others.

This act of Jesus around that table in Jerusalem has incredible significance. It foreshadowed the deep cleansing from sin that he would soon realize as he humbled himself to death for his people. It gives an example of what true power, and true love, and true life really look like. Unlike us, Jesus wasn't constrained by the power relations that operated in the world of his day. His disregard of convention in an act of radical service held out a new way of life. He died under the powers of the world, but in his resurrection from the dead his life on earth and his teaching were vindicated. He truly lived through death and points the way to a new pattern of life. This is the life of the City of God that can be lived even within the midst of the City of Man.

Through the book we have talked about the practices of life that are the ways of flourishing in the digital world. We have considered issues of identity, relationships, time, sex and knowledge. In each chapter we have highlighted practices of life that go with the grain of God's design for the world. To see these practices embodied, we need look no further than Jesus Christ.

When his identity was challenged and he might have despaired, Jesus practised deep trust in God, retreating for times of prayer and fully engaging in a life given to serving the people. He didn't depend on the affirmation of his followers to make him who he was. And a good job too, since his followers would later desert him and join in condemning him. He knew who he was in the eyes of his Father and so had an assurance and security that went with his life of faith, hope and love.

Jesus withdrew from the crowds to spend time alone with God in prayer, but his was no isolated life. He had the strongest of relationships with his followers and was never aloof. He welcomed children and was friends with prostitutes and tax collectors (the social outsiders of the day). He didn't ignore the issues that the modern world places under the categories of class, gender and race, but neither was he bound by the divisions of his day. He noticed people, listened and welcomed them. His practice of hospitality brought people together in a new and wonderful unity.

Jesus learned how to live well in time. He cultivated patience, waiting on God and so not grasping in the present what belonged to the future. That meant that he had what so many people in the modern world are chasing. In the midst of the busyness of a public ministry where he was always on the move and constantly called on by others, Jesus always had time. How was it possible? The answer is found in the way Jesus, relying on God's Spirit, had learnt the lesson with which humankind has always struggled. In the Garden of Eden, Adam and Eve couldn't wait for God to fulfil his promises and seized what was not yet theirs. Wandering in the wilderness, the people of Israel couldn't come to terms with the fact that God gives his gifts in his own time. They grumbled against God, refusing to trust him. At the outset of his public ministry, Jesus spent forty days fasting in the desert. He was tempted by Satan, who offered him all the kingdoms of the world and their glory there and then. Jesus only had to bow down and worship him (Matthew 4:8–9). He waited. With a firm hope in God to give him what he needed at just the right time, Jesus lived without anxiety but in dependence on his heavenly Father. In the example of Jesus we see a way of relating to time that replaces haste with hope and transforms fretful anxiety into purposeful activity.

What about sex? Surely this is one area in which Jesus really can't be our model of life lived well? Being single, to state the obvious for a moment, Jesus never had sex. But perhaps that is exactly the reason he is such an important example for us in a sex-obsessed world. Think, for a moment, what good sex demands. How about trust, commitment, love, devotion? How about purity, and chastity? Chastity (the practice of abstaining from sex) isn't much discussed these days and less often practised, but chastity is fundamental to sex because it is the practice that allows us to have something to give. Sex in our culture is about getting. The world thinks of the best sex as where both people get what they want. The problem is that this approach to sex undermines the relationship by using the other person as a means to our own ends.

In John 4, Jesus meets a Samaritan woman at a well. She is all on her own, fetching water in the heat of the day. She has been excluded from society. Breaking all social conventions, Jesus speaks to her with great compassion. He tells her he knows why she's an outcast. She has had a string of failed relationships and is now too ashamed to show her face in public. We aren't told anything about the details and who is to blame, but the woman seems to have been used and is now used up. From one encounter with Jesus the woman finds refreshment and is restored. Like a well that is cracked, the 'getting' culture cannot hold water. It treats people like disposable objects and always leaves us thirsty to get more. Jesus related to women deeply and personally, he wasn't aloof or embarrassed, and yet he was perfectly chaste – he had learnt to appreciate sex as God's gift.

The final area of life we considered was the area of wisdom and knowledge. In a society where knowledge was power, Jesus left the religious teachers staggered by his wisdom. He studied the Scriptures from a young age and the way he understood the Old Testament bears witness to the way he had worked to learn and to love God's Word. And yet he refused to use this knowledge to secure his status in the world. He left lawyers and religious teachers furious at the fact that he refused to play their power game, sharing his wisdom freely with the most marginalized members of society. For Jesus, knowledge went with wisdom and service and love. And that meant using all he knew in loving service of others and for the surpassing glory of God. He didn't avoid confrontation, boldly speaking truth to power. But he didn't enter into debates to score points. He asked questions as well as gave answers. He was the model of contextualization, speaking to people rather than at them.

The early Christian leader Irenaeus of Lyons famously taught that 'the glory of God is man fully alive'.[6] In Jesus Christ we see that glory revealed. It is as we look at Jesus Christ that we see in practice a wonderful vision of new life for our digital world.

And if we come to Jesus, we can participate in it ourselves. The life we see in Jesus can be the life we know, transforming our lives from within, renewing our relationship with creation and with others, making our world sing.

At its worst, technology takes its place in the City of Man as the mechanical means to further the clenched human hand of power. But the City of Man doesn't win. And it doesn't win because Jesus has taken its worst. At the cross he was crushed by the dark power of the world, the dark power of sin that resides in the heart of humankind. And on the third day he rose in victory to herald the beginning of a new world, the City of God, which will one day fill the earth.

The truly human life is the life that Jesus lived. And it is the life that Jesus gave. And in raising him from the dead, it is the life that was given to him by God, the glorious reward for his work on earth.

The way to enjoy true life is to come to Jesus Christ in repentance and faith. It is to release the clenched fist of power to hold open hands that are willing to receive the gift that he offers – the gift that is his life counting for us, and his life working within us by the power of the Holy Spirit.

In John 10:10 Jesus says of his people, 'I came that they may have life and have it abundantly.'

As we look to Jesus we see a picture of what could be. As we come to Jesus in repentance and faith, his life becomes our life, and that vision becomes a transforming vision for flourishing in our digital world.

Notes

Introduction

1. Charles Taylor, *A Secular Age* (Harvard University Press, 2007), ch. 16.

Chapter 1 Just a tool?

1. A good place to start is with Tim Keller's excellent book, *The Reason for God: Belief in an Age of Skepticism* (Dutton, 2008).
2. Martin Heidegger, *The Question Concerning Technology and Other Essays* (Garland, 1977), p. 4.
3. *The Telegraph*, Review section, 6 December 2014.
4. http://news.bbc.co.uk/1/hi/technology/4132752.stm
5. Neil Postman, *Amusing Ourselves to Death: Public Discourse in the Age of Show Business* (Penguin, 2005), p. 8.
6. Nicholas Carr, *The Shallows: How the Internet Is Changing the Way We Think, Read and Remember* (Atlantic Books, 2010), pp. 44–46.
7. Carr, *The Shallows*, p. 47.
8. Ralph Waldo Emerson (1803–82), 'Ode, Inscribed to William H. Channing' (1899).
9. Steve Jobs, Stanford commencement speech, 2005; http://news.stanford.edu/news/2005/june15/jobs-061505.html
10. Nicolas de Condorcet (1743–94), 'The Future Progress of the Human Mind' (1795).
11. Nick Bostrom, 'A History of Transhumanist Thought' (2005); http://www.nickbostrom.com/papers/history.pdf

Chapter 2 What's the story?

1. Catherine Bray, 'The ten sci-fi movie inventions we wish were real', 22 July 2014; http://www.timeout.com/london/film/sci-fi-movie-inventions

2. C. S. Lewis, *Mere Christianity* (Collins, 1988), p. 35.

3. Alasdair MacIntyre, *After Virtue: A Study in Moral Theory*, 3rd edition (Notre Dame Press, 2007).

4. Johnny Ryan, *The History of the Internet and the Digital Future* (Reaktion Books, 2010), pp. 55–56.

5. Augustine, *City of God: Concerning the City of God against the Pagans*, trans. Henry Bettenson (Penguin, 1984), 19.13.

6. Brian Brock, *Christian Ethics in a Technological Age* (Eerdmans, 2010), p. 225.

7. Brock, *Christian Ethics*, p. 207.

8. These areas were taken from Oliver O'Donovan's book, *Self, World and Time: Ethics as Theology* (Eerdmans, 2013).

9. Tom Warren, 'Bill Gates admits Control-Alt-Delete mistake, blames IBM', *The Verge* online, 26 September 2013; http://www.theverge.com/2013/9/26/4772680/bill-gates-admits-ctrl-alt-del-was-a-mistake

10. William Blake (1757–1827), 'Jerusalem' (1810).

11. Oliver O'Donovan, *Resurrection and Moral Order: An Outline for Evangelical Ethics* (Apollos, 2001), p. 55.

12. 'Holy Spirit, Living Breath of God', words and music by Keith Getty and Stuart Townend, © 2006 Thankyou Music.

Chapter 4 I tweet therefore I am

1. 'Facebook is bad for you: get a life!', *The Economist*, 17 August 2013; http://www.economist.com/news/science-and-technology/21583593-using-social-network-seems-make-people-more-miserable-get-life

2. Dave Eggers, *The Circle* (Hamish Hamilton, 2013), p. 21.

3. John Calvin, *Institutes of the Christian Religion*, 1.3.8.

4. 'David Foster Wallace in his own words', *Intelligent Life* magazine, 19 September 2008.

5. Dietrich Bonhoeffer, 'Who Am I?', taken from *Letters and Papers from Prison* © Dietrich Bonhoeffer, trans. Eberhard Bethge (SCM Press, 1971) and reproduced by permission of Hymns Ancient & Modern Ltd.

Chapter 5 The social network

1. Paul Hoffman (ed.), 'The Tao of the IETF: A Novice's Guide to the Internet Engineering Task Force', 1st edition (2009); http://www.ietf.org/tao.html

2. http://news.bbc.co.uk/1/hi/technology/4132752.stm

3. Craig Detweiler, *iGods: How Technology Shapes Our Spiritual and Social Lives* (Brazos Press, 2013), p. 143.

4. Sherry Turkle, *Alone Together: Why We Expect More from Technology and Less from Each Other* (Basic Books, 2011).

5. Michael Horton, *The Christian Faith: A Systematic Theology for Pilgrims on The Way* (Zondervan, 2011), p. 380.

6. Dietrich Bonhoeffer, *Life Together*, ed. Geffrey B. Kelly, trans. Daniel W. Bloesch and James H. Burtness (Fortress Press, 2005), p. 37.

Chapter 6 Real time

1. Richard Powers, *The Paris Review Book for Planes, Trains, Elevators and Waiting Rooms* (Picador, 2004).

2. Lorenzo C. Simpson, *Technology, Time, and the Conversations of Modernity* (Routledge, 1995), p. 23.

3. C. S. Lewis, quoted in Alister E. McGrath, *The Intellectual World of C. S. Lewis* (Wiley-Blackwell, 2014), p. 42.

4. C. S. Lewis, *The Last Battle* (HarperCollins, 1984), p. 228.

5. See for example Jessica Kleiman, 'How multitasking hurts your brain (and your effectiveness at work)', *Forbes* magazine, 15 January 2013; http://www.forbes.com/sites/work-in-

progress/2013/01/15/how-multitasking-hurts-your-brain-
and-your-effectiveness-at-work

6. Nick Bilton, 'Steve Jobs was a low-tech parent', *New York
Times*, 10 September 2014; http://www.nytimes.
com/2014/09/11/fashion/steve-jobs-apple-was-a-low-tech-
parent.html?_r=1

Chapter 7 Virtual sex

1. Jack Sommers, 'Sexting could earn teenagers criminal
record and place on sex offenders' register', *The Huffington
Post UK*, 23 July 2014; http://www.huffingtonpost.co.uk/
2014/07/23/sexting-teenagers-criminal-records_n_5612399.
html

2. Michel Foucault, *The History of Sexuality*, vol. 1 (Penguin,
2008), pp. 8–9.

3. Kinsey Institute: Advancing Sexual Health and Knowledge
Worldwide; http://www.kinseyinstitute.org/resources/
FAQ.html#internet (accessed 11 December 2014).

4. Al Cooper, *Sex and the Internet: A Guide Book for Clinicians*
(Routledge, 2002), p. 4.

5. Eric Schmidt and Jared Cohen, *The New Digital Age: Reshaping
the Future of People, Nations and Business* (John Murray, 2013),
p. 67.

6. Brian Brock, *Christian Ethics in a Technological Age* (Eerdmans,
2010), p. 332.

7. John Wyatt, *Matters of Life and Death*, 2nd edition (IVP,
2009).

8. National Institute of Health and Clinical Excellence figures,
quoted by 'Beating Eating Disorders' website; http://
www.b-eat.co.uk/about-beat/media-centre/facts-and-figures
(accessed 11 December 2014).

9. Wellcome Trust, 'Survey examines changes in sexual
behaviour and attitudes in Britain', 26 November 2013;

http://www.wellcome.ac.uk/News/Media-office/Press-releases/2013/Press-releases/WTP054816.htm

10. Michael Inbar, '"Sexting" bullying cited in teen suicide', *Today* news online, 12 February 2009; http://www.today.com/id/34236377/ns/today-today_news/t/sexting-bullying-cited-teens-suicide/#.VInfmWSsVXY

11. Martin Daubney, 'The lads' mag I edited turned a generation on to porn – and now I'm a father I bitterly regret it: a remarkable confession from the longest-serving editor of *Loaded*', *Daily Mail*, 8 June 2012. Read online (discretion advised) at http://www.dailymail.co.uk/news/article-2156593/The-lads-mag-I-edited-turned-generation-porn--Im-father-I-bitterly-regret-A-remarkable-confession-longest-serving-editor-Loaded.html#ixzz3LbZtB56U

12. Ibid.

13. For help with pornography see Tim Chester, *Captured by a Better Vision: Living Porn Free* (IVP, 2010). For help with eating disorders we recommend Emma Scrivener, *A New Name: Grace and Healing for Anorexia* (IVP, 2012).

14. Johanna Blakley, 'Social media and the end of gender', filmed December 2010. Available online at http://www.ted.com/talks/johanna_blakley_social_media_and_the_end_of_gender?language=en#t-276720

15. Rhiannon Williams, 'Facebook's 71 gender options come to UK users', *Telegraph* online, 27 June 2014; http://www.telegraph.co.uk/technology/facebook/10930654/Facebooks-71-gender-options-come-to-UK-users.html

16. Sam Jones, 'Media "influence" adolescent sex', *Guardian* newspaper, 22 March 2006. Available online at http://www.theguardian.com/media/2006/mar/22/pressandpublishing.broadcasting

17. See particularly chapters 1 and 2 on this.

18. E.g. Mark 8:2–38; John 9:1–41.

19. Words by John Newton (1725–1807). The words have recently been reset by Sovereign Grace Praise in 'The Look', *Upward: The Bob Kauflin Hymns Project* (2001).

Chapter 8 Searching for knowledge

1. Murad Ahmed, 'Google, the next generation, will be beaming up everwhere', *The Times*, 22 October 2012.
2. Philip Howard, Aiden Duffy et al., 'Opening closed regimes: what was the role of social media during the Arab Spring?', *Project on Information Technology and Political Islam* (University of Washington, 2011).
3. Richard Alleyne, 'Welcome to the information age – 174 newspapers a day', *Telegraph*, 11 February 2011 (based on an eighty-five-page newspaper).
4. *The Week* magazine, 7 August 2006.
5. T. S. Eliot, 'The Rock' (1934).
6. See particularly *De Trinitate* (On the Trinity), books 12–14.
7. Itiel E. Dror, 'Perceptual, cognitive, and psychological elements involved in expert identification', in Alan McRoberts (ed.), *Friction Ridge Sourcebook* (2006).
8. Ibid.
9. 'These inner attitudes of the human heart determined the will's direction which then had power over the other faculty of reasoning as well . . . the passions of the heart ultimately determined human conduct, an affection could only be "overcome by a more vehement affection".' Quote from Ashley Null, *Thomas Cranmer's Doctrine of Repentance: Renewing the Power of Love* (Oxford University Press, 2000), pp. 100–101.

Conclusion: Truly human

1. Martin Heidegger, *The Question Concerning Technology and Other Essays* (Garland, 1977), p. 4.

2. Steve Jobs, quoted in 'Steve Jobs: Stanford commencement address, June 2005', *Guardian* online, 9 October 2011; http://www.theguardian.com/technology/2011/oct/09/steve-jobs-stanford-commencement-address

3. Heidi A. Campbell and Antonio C. La Pastina, 'How the iPhone became divine: new media, religion and the intertextual circulation of meaning', *New Media & Society* 12.7 (2010), pp. 1191–1207.

4. Olivia Goldhill, 'Happy birthday Steve Jobs: how Apple disciples still worship the modern messiah', *Telegraph* online, 17 August 2015; http://www.telegraph.co.uk/technology/steve-jobs/11432949/Happy-birthday-Steve-Jobs-how-Apple-disciples-still-worship-the-modern-messiah.html

5. Walter Isaacson, *Steve Jobs: The Exclusive Biography* (Little, Brown, 2011), p. 43.

6. Irenaeus, *Against Heresies*, 4.34.